To

F.I.

thanks for the "good stuff"

The Cryptics

Foreword

Birth of a Notion

In the winter of 1986, within the snow-covered environs of Ewen Park in the Bronx, the birth of a notion took place. Jim Mannion and myself decided to channel our rabid fulminations onto paper and found a newsletter of political and miscellaneous musings.

The Progressive Pragmatist was born, with the first issue seeing the light of day in June, 1986. My partner and I, after heated debate, lifted our catchy name from then-New York Governor Mario Cuomo's self-description of his political philosophy. Cuomo didn't want to be called a "liberal." In the heart of the Reagan Era, he thought it pejorative. He preferred the moniker "progressive pragmatist."

He fooled nobody.

Looking back almost a decade later, the fledgling years of *The Progressive Pragmatist* both amuse and horrify me. The philosophy Jim and I enunciated in those early days was distinctly left-leaning and appropriately cliché-laden.

The intensive Cardinal O'Connor and Catholic Church bashing makes me cringe a little. I've completely exorcised my post-Catholic school demons. I dare say I'd send my kids (if I had any) to Catholic school. The NYC Public School System is a backed-up sewer rife with violence and peppered with bizarre "multi-cultural" flimflam.

The Progressive Pragmatist, for the better, matured over the years. In the mid-to-late 1980's, the right-wingers on the political landscape were clearly the bad guys. The fundamentalist fomentations blowing from the Bible Belt

AMERICA OFF-LINE

REAGAN TO O.J.

by Nicholas J. Nigro and James Mannion
annotated by James Mannion

CRYPTIC PRESS BRONX, N.Y.

Published by Cryptic Press, Inc.
One Riverdale Avenue, Suite 452
Bronx, New York 10463

Library of Congress Catalog Number: 95-71613

ISBN: 1-887775-01-3

First Printing: 1996

Printed in the United States of America

Cover photographs from authors' private collections.

were achieving a frightening legitimacy in the Reagan and Bush White Houses.

Contrarily, today, the so-called political left houses the deleterious demagogues polluting the political arena. *Political Correctness* is epidemic, as legitimate policy debates are stifled by accusations of racism.

Upon Barry Goldwater's retirement from politics, he penned an autobiography titled *With No Apologies.* His political philosophy has evolved, and he is no longer the "In Your Heart You Know He's Right" candidate of 1964. Nor are we the 1986 *Progressive Pragmatist.*

No apologies necessary or forthcoming. It's part of the maturity process. So, come fly with us on our little sojourn from Ronald Reagan's America to Bill Clinton's. Or is it O.J. Simpson's?

Nicholas J. Nigro
Bronx, New York
October 1995

Prologue:

Today

1995

What follows is an excerpt from the last issue of The Progressive Pragmatist.

Juice II

"True Crime" makes for compelling viewing. The O.J. Simpson trial is the most celebrated of its kind in many years. "The Trial of the Century," no doubt you've heard it called.

O.J.'s celebrity status was waning long before the murders. The athlete's glory days were a thing of the past. His Hertz commercials were off the air. His "lame actor" status was certifiable.

The circumstances of the murder and the riveting Bronco chase have made O.J. more famous than his pigskin heroics. He has finally reached the *top of the charts*.

O.J.'s recently published book, live from incarceration, proclaims his innocence and his love for the late Nicole. He also, in the best *Bartyles and James* tradition, thanks the public for their support.

O.J.'s venom is saved for the media, for which he now expresses extreme revulsion. He vows never to return to a profession of such ill-repute.

So, what will O.J. do if he is acquitted of the heinous double murder? He won't be peddling bogus arthritis cures or shilling ubiquitous work-out videos. It's not likely he'll be welcome on the set of *Naked Gun 4 1/4* (they're a bold bunch, but. . .). What will he do?

O.J. will discover his lost black heritage, and renounce the white society that has long used and abused him. He'll cuddle up to Louie Farrakhan and his bow-tied muscle. He'll don a fez and celebrate Kwaanza.

You heard it here first.

Nicholas J. Nigro

As this book was about to go to press, O.J. Simpson was acquitted, so NJN's prediction may have come to pass by the time you read this.

With the 1996 Presidential election less than a year away, here is an NJN piece, the prescience of which is yet to be determined.

Handicapping the 1996 Presidential Suspects

Republicans

Bob Dole:

Looks increasingly like a wax figure. Compare the 1976 Dole, Gerald Ford's running mate, to Dole today. At 71, he's just too old and too compromised as a politician to be taken seriously. He has already spoken of serving only one term. He may be the front-runner, but he's beginning to bruise and rot.

Phil Gramm:

Raving right-winger who, to his credit, is not wearing a wig and hasn't had his weasly face pressed and tucked. He'd be an impersonator's dream with his Texas drawl and sniveling snarl. Another Vietnam War supporter and no-show, who had the audacity to knock Clinton as a "draft dodger."

Jack Kemp:

Wants to help poor people. This attitude doesn't play well in Republican primaries. Won't run because he says he needs to raise $20 million by this time next year. Why does the pick of the Republican litter pass up this opportunity? Is it too late for him to change his mind?

Arlen Specter:

A moderate Republican who must want to be on the ticket as Vice-President. If he seriously believes he has a shot, he's seriously delusional.

Lamar Alexander:

Former Tennessee Governor, Secretary of Education, and Washington insider, running as an outsider. Announced his candidacy wearing a flannel shirt. Then he put on a suit and headed for New Hampshire.

Dan Quayle:

Dumb in 1988; dumber in 1996. No wonder he's already out.

Pete Wilson:

If dullness was a Presidential attribute, he'd win hands down. Big champion of Proposition 187 in California.

Pat Buchanan:

Speaking of Proposition 187, the former CNN pundit wants to build a Berlin Wall along our southern border. Certainly adds spice to the race with his strident posturing and goofy laugh.

Bob Dornan:

If this California Congressman were a dog, he'd be put to sleep. He's rabid. The most horrifying man in Congress.

Richard Lugar:

A man of integrity with foreign policy credentials. Nobody cares.

Democrats

Jesse Jackson:

This publicity-craving blowhard will run, maybe on a third party ticket just to thwart Clinton. Loud-mouths like Jackson benefit by having a Republican in the White House. Gives them more to shout about.

President Bill Clinton:

He doesn't look the part with his weak mouth and blow-dried coiffure. His background is minus war-time heroics. He doesn't even have a true rags-to-riches story, only a tepid, chicken-fried white trash tale of an unhappy childhood and crapulent step-father. And yes, he has consorted with women other than Hillary. Naughty Bill and his many airheads.

More than halfway through his Presidency, he could be evaluated as a fair President. The deficit is down, the economy is performing better than status quo, and we are at peace.

That used to be enough to re-elect Presidents.

Bob Casey:

Former Governor of Pennsylvania and pro-life Democrat. Might want to rattle Clinton a little on the right in his own party. A little rattling can't hurt, particularly with the Democratic Party floundering as it is.

Sam Nunn:

It would be refreshing if Clinton were seriously challenged in his own party. The President's character woes are so elephantine that most of us would rather see him return to an Arkansas law practice.

Independents

Colin Powell:

A man of integrity and stature, who has no party and hasn't taken a stand on the issues. Hence, a popular favorite.

Ross Perot:

Still whining about everything under the sun, and richer than ever. Is Fruit Loops II in the offing?

NJN

After years of increasing disillusionment, NJN finally puts the last nail in the coffin of his hero-worship of former New York Governor Mario Cuomo, who future generations will probably best remember as the man who coined the term "Progressive Pragmatist."

Shut Up for Me, Mr. C.

Mario Cuomo is now a private citizen. New Yorkers bid adieu to their voluble former Governor this past November.

Having once been a Cuomo-phile, his passing from politics proved bittersweet. This time I cast my lot with an opponent of his. Not George Pataki (I couldn't bring myself to vote for the GOP candidate). I voted for an independent named Thomas Golisano, a man with big bucks and a stylish white 'do.

Golisano was not a serious contender, hence on election night I maintained a cynical "it doesn't make a difference" stance. If Ol' Baggy Eyes got in for another four years — so what! As the night wore on, however, my facade crumbled, and I relished the thought of no more Mario.

My only concern was Mayor Giuliani's endorsement of the incumbent, and the possible fallout for the city if Cuomo lost. The mayor courageously crossed party lines and endorsed a man who is anathema to rank-and-file Republicans, because he felt Pataki was an empty suit, and the hand-picked puppet of Senator Sleaze — Al D'Amato. While agreeing with Rudy's assessment of Pataki, I could no longer countenance the pompous reign of Mario Cuomo.

In any event, Cuomo lost and Giuliani is a pariah

in *Republican Town*. This attests to the Mayor's character. He'll survive. What counts is that Cuomo is out of a government job — at last!

Watching Cuomo's political post-mortem hasn't been pretty. It has revealed just how out of touch he is; how anachronistic he has become. Needless to say, the introspective Hamlet doesn't see it. He feels the Empire State electorate is comprised largely of "ignoramuses" for failing to reward his many "accomplishments" with a fourth term.

Eleven years ago, Cuomo electrified the Democratic Convention with his stirring oratory. Where did he go wrong? Key: He never translated his lofty verbiage into public policy. Sure, Mario bitterly laments that today's politicians won't talk about "compassion," for fear of being defeated at the polls. With him, it always comes down to the cold, cruel electorate — the "ignoramuses." This attitude is classic Cuomo.

Mario believes that he among politicians is the *King of Compassion*, and that he was evicted from his mansion in Albany because his heart was too big. The truth, Mario, is that your mouth was the only thing too big. Your platitudes about love and compassion have degenerated into a sycophantic brand of white paternalism.

Yes, your "son of immigrants" story was inspiring, but it doesn't jibe with your present day philosophy. Cuomo's parents came to America and worked dawn to dusk to make a better life for themselves and their family. Mario made it through law school, was discriminated against in his job search because of his Italian heritage, and ultimately became the Governor of New York State. The good, the bad, and the ugly (and without government assistance).

Cuomo elegantly champions the lower classes — and

they do need champions. Where he goes wrong, in this era of big government red ink, is in not insisting on even a speck of accountability in the dispensation of governmental largesse.

When the Governor left office after 12 years, he didn't return to his old neighborhood in Hollis, Queens. He moved into a door-manned high-rise on Manhattan's fashionable Upper West Side. The middle class, who once gave Mario their support, turned their backs on the "child of immigrants," because he turned his back on them a long time ago. He insulted these decent, hard-working people, and continues to do so, by inferring that they're all a bunch of ignorant bigots for feeling angry at the decline of their once proud city and state.

Mario, you and your ilk have swapped your souls for the surreal life of politics. Come on, be my neighbor in the Bronx for while, or else do me a big favor and **Shut Up!**

Well, it looks like NJN won't be a guest on Mario's new radio program, which he rather smugly says is "thought radio," not "talk radio."

The Return:

Beginning at The End

1994

We're starting at the end of our epoch and traveling backward in this anthology, because we feel our best stuff came as we evolved and matured as writers and as men. After a consistent, steady run from 1986-1992, we stopped the presses due to waning enthusiasm and a desire to extend our range. Due to popular demand, NJN brought the Progressive Pragmatist back for a limited run, with limited participation from yours truly. (I wrote one new piece, and two Mannion "classics" were re-printed.) Consider this chapter akin to a Gilligan's Island reunion movie.

Number 42 Looks Just Like You

The Clinton Presidency's infancy was a colossal embarrassment. For those of us who cheered a Democrat in the White House at long last, his initial performance was a tough pill to swallow.

It appeared Bill Clinton was a Jimmy Carter redux. Overconfident, arrogant, and in over his head. Why did he make gays in the military the centerpiece of his fledgling Presidency? Why did he insist on filling jobs based on quotas instead of competence?

On second thought, my apologies to Jimmy Carter. His honeymoon was an actual honeymoon. When he walked down Pennsylvania Avenue in January 1977, the American people's goodwill shone upon him. Not so with Bill Clinton.

Clinton was, and is, *Slick Willie*, to many people. Those who despised him were intent on seeing him fail. Then something miraculous happened. Republican David Gergen went to work for Bill Clinton, wresting control from the know-it-all Yuppies who were wreaking havoc behind the scenes of the new administration.

Then suddenly Clinton metamorphosed into a President. His stature grew with each passing day and his initiatives went places.

The Republican obstructionists, led by Bob *(Please Fall on your Pen!)* Dole were looking more and more like . . . Republican obstructionists, bent only on seeing Clinton fail.

Enter the Clinton proposed universal health plan. A bold proposal and the reason many of us pulled the lever for Clinton. We wanted positive activism in addressing society's ills. The health care system is ludicrous. Few politicians have had the guts to take on the greedy capitalists who've been feeding off other's misfortunes. Clinton has made a first step towards universal coverage.

There's little doubt that Clinton is more in touch with Regular Joes than his recent GOP predecessors, but he's a true politician. The fact that he wasn't born with a trust fund in his name offers us a sliver of hope that some good may come out of his Presidency.

Year One gives the President a solid B grade. A move toward national health care, NAFTA passage, a semi-serious budget, a big crime bill and the passage of the Brady law, are, we hope, harbingers of things to come.

NJN

The title is a rather "cryptic" reference to a Twilight Zone episode. It indicates NJN's gradual shift in interest from the gritty world of politics to the ethereal realm of classic television.

NJN's political prescience leaves something to be desired. As of this writing, there is no national health care, something I'm reminded of every time I have to write out a check for $511.14 to my local HIP, wait for two hours to see an indifferent, bureaucrat-doctor, who feels my groin and hands me a stool sample kit.

In this next piece, NJN takes on the erstwhile Rainbow Curriculum of the New York City Public School System, a program which, like the Rainbow Coalition that inspired it, sent out the clear message: Heterosexual White Males Need Not Apply.

Somewhere Over the Rainbow

When Bill Clinton was President-elect, a list being circulated of prospective Secretaries of Education included the name of then New York City Schools Chancellor Joseph Fernandez. He was on the list, it's fair to say, because he was a Latino.

For New Yorkers, the notion of Fernandez going national was absurd. His intellect was not in question. He was credited, albeit marginally, with improving the city's rueful school system. Where he erred was in promoting his so-called "Rainbow Curriculum." Controversial in the Big Apple, it was considered down-right deviant everywhere else. It kowtowed to ultra-left special interests and was the flip side of Pat Robertson's Christian Coalition.

I don't know how one teaches "tolerance." It's the same as trying to legislate "morality." By having first-graders read a book called *Heather's Two Mommies*, Fernandez and associates reasoned this would show six-year-olds that some of their peers are raised in lesbian households. I don't know anyone from a "two mom" family (and I'm a New Yorker!). They exist in infinitesimal numbers, and that's fine by me. The numbers of two mom (and two dad) families are statistically insignificant, and don't merit being the subject of a first grade reader. *Heather's Single Mommy* is a more timely topic for today's city kid.

Fernandez was ousted for following the Rainbow at the expense of reading, writing and arithmetic. *See Spot Run* just wouldn't cut it with these kooky educators.

Tolerance of other races, religions, and alternative lifestyles cannot be taught in a heavy-handed manner. Tolerance develops in developed minds. Well-educated, intelligent kids are tolerant of others. Lunkheads are intolerant boobs, whether they read *Heather's Two Mommies* or not.

If the Joe Fernandez's of the world would concentrate their efforts on what's worked in the past, and would not be intimidated by extremist pressure groups, the school systems in all our cities would be better equipped in educating. Which, ostensibly, is their purpose.

Besides, after *Heather's Two Mommies*, why not *Jubal's Twenty-Two Wives?* After all, polygamy is an alternative lifestyle, too.

NJN

My only new contribution to "The Return" was a fluff piece I could have written in my sleep. I have been accused of quickly degenerating into a self-parody by my vociferous critics. This is unfair and inaccurate criticism. Read on, my friends, and you'll see I was a self-parody from Day One.

Financially Secure

A recent perusal of the personal ads in several New York City and Westchester dailies revealed a disturbing and mercenary trend among single women, who, in these liberated times, shouldn't be so calculating and unromantic. The most commonly repeated prerequisite in their man-hunt is that the fellow be "financially secure."

This is understandable if the woman is trying to eliminate freeloaders and shiftless no-goodniks from her list of potential suitors. I believe that "financially secure" has more gold-digging implications.

Even as a recent addition to America's "downsized" subculture, I am financially secure. I have a comfortable stash in my savings account, and a hefty 401K that I rolled-over into an interest-bearing IRA. Even on my small weekly unemployment checks, I can pay my bills.

If however, I am asked to provide a lavish lifestyle of fine dining, Hampton jaunts, and stylish baubles, bangles, and beads for a demanding lover, I will quickly become financially insecure.

Take me as I am, ladies — a dashing young poet, and rising star on the literary scene, and attentive, passionate lover. Join me in these exciting salad days, a prelude to an affluent maturity.

Shallow bimbos need not apply.

JM

That was written in May 1994. At the time of this writing, the unemployment checks have stopped, the savings have dwindled, and the IRA is losing money.
BUY THIS BOOK, PLEASE!!!

The "Pathmark-Guy" Syndrome

Ten years ago, the popular TV series, *Little House on the Prairie*, ended its long run with a telemovie in which the townspeople blow up their homes and businesses, rather than turn them over to a despicable businessman (who, it turned out, owned the land they stood on). The greedy capitalist was played by a familiar character actor, most recognized as the commercial pitch-man for the Pathmark supermarket chain.

After the episode aired, Pathmark received hundreds of calls from distressed consumers. How could they have such an evil man in their employ? Can him before the next tuna fish sale, they demanded. The Pathmark brass were understandably rattled and considered dumping the guy, who was likewise unnerved. He needed the job.

It's not only TV and movies that confuse people as to what is real and what's make believe. The "Pathmark-Guy" Syndrome is pervasive. The two hottest creatures currently on radio are the grotesque Howard Stern and the porcine Rush Limbaugh.

Stern is a "shock jock" whose schtick is being ultra-tasteless. He's presently a candidate for Governor of New York, having been nominated by the craven Libertarian Party, believe it or not, on a platform of fixing potholes and frying no-goodniks.

What's bizarre is not that people would vote for him. A vote for gargoyle Stern as a vote for none-of-the-above, is appealing in a perverse way. But some of Stern's supporters are championing their candidate on his merits. The man is an entertainer!

And then there's Rush. His legions of obsequious ditto-heads are convinced he'd make a great President. They don't seem to grasp that the man is a talk-show host and comedian. He performs clever bits on occasion, quite amusing in their political incorrectness. This hardly speaks to his qualities as a Chief Executive. He sits in a glass bubble and slobbers into a microphone as flatterers and sycophants spew their love for him.

Not too long ago, I received a call from the Cuomo for Governor reelection campaign, asking for $100, then $50, then $25. They got nothing, then warned me of the prospect of losing Cuomo's "compassion" to a cold-hearted Republican (Stern wasn't mentioned).

What the Cuomo people didn't know was that they were talking to a prospective gubernatorial candidate with a platform of his own:

- lower taxes for everybody
- schools that educate
- clean air to breathe and water to drink
- tough anti-crime measures, including the return of public flogging

It can't miss.

NJN

NJN makes yet another TV analogy in this piece, but finally goes over the deep end in the next, renouncing his position as political pundit, preferring to romp in the Neverland of reruns.

Say It Ain't So, Ben

Dan Quayle made a now infamous speech while on the campaign trail in 1992. It's remembered for its *Murphy Brown* reference, when the Veep lamented that the unmarried TV character was having a baby. The content of the rest of the speech on the need for family values was lost in the ridicule of Quayle for taking on a fictional character.

President Clinton resurrected the Quayle speech recently, lauding its basic message. Instead of *Murphy Brown*, Clinton could have commented on the tragic fate of Ben Cartwright.

We learned in the telemovie, *Bonanza Rides Again*, that the grand patriarch of the Ponderosa, who we once thought epitomized virtue and values, was a failure as a father.

He died with his *long-time male companion* at his side, and none of his sons. We found out that Hoss had drowned trying to save someone. That was just like him! What we would never have guessed is that he had impregnated a woman a short time before the accident. Hoss, Jr. grew up thinking his dad had abandoned him. Could Ol' Hoss have been taking a few extra risks because of the shameful news he had for Paw?

Little Joe was likewise deceased. He died charging up San Juan Hill with Teddy Roosevelt's Rough Riders. A very *Cartwright* thing to do. Meanwhile, his son grew up resenting his absentee father.

Adam, the only living son, was over in Australia. His son found him to be an uncommunicative taskmaster, and tough act to follow. Even with the Ponderosa in jeopardy of falling into a greedy developer's hands, Adam didn't care enough to take a ship home.

Ben Cartwright, remember, was a single parent. He failed. He thought his boys would stay on the ranch forever. He thought he was immortal because his sons would carry on, but the sons couldn't wait to leave the nest! Perhaps in a stable two-parent environment, things might have turned out differently.

NJN

NJN took a look back at the long run of The Progressive Pragmatist, and winced at some of his early opinions. He then drafted this piece about his changing tune over the years. What follows is essentially an apology for the rest of the book.

Regrets, We've Had a Few. . .

Mario Cuomo:

The man coined the phrase *Progressive Pragmatist*, calling it a substitute for the much-maligned "liberal" moniker. I liked Cuomo in his political infancy. His charisma, a refreshing blend of candor and vigor, was more than welcome on the political landscape. Cuomo was *real* at first. Sadly, 12 years in Albany have tarnished his pristine veneer. He has devolved into a pompous blowhard. Though still capable of packing an oratory wallop, he is incapable of courageously governing. His latest book, *More Than Words* is a chronology of his greatest speeches. The regrettable irony is that Cuomo, the politician, is not more than words.

Jerry Brown:

I briefly got caught up in this flake's 1-800-insurgent campaign for President. I never expected him to win, but I thought he'd at least avoid pandering. I cast my primary vote for him, but by that time I'd already had my fill of the man who reinvents himself every hour.

Cardinal O'Connor:

We frequently bashed this prelate with the funny hat and expensive rings. Yes, John Cardinal O'Connor served as the *P.P.* whipping boy for many years. He didn't rate being the scapegoat for our parochial school trauma. Admittedly, however, it was fun. Sorry, Eminence.

1992-1993

Though we offer our sincerest condolences to former President Reagan and his family, please note that we keenly observed his Alzheimer's several years before his hand-written announcement to the American people.

Here We Go Again

After the leader of the free world vomited on the Japanese Prime Minister, he flew home to the friendly confines of these United States, heading straight for New Hampshire, home of the first Presidential primary, to talk to flesh-and-blood Americans about bread-and-butter issues.

He was a tad excitable, trying once again to prove that he's a "regular guy" who empathizes with the plight of the common man and woman.

This journey to the Granite State was the unofficial 1992 Bush political send-off, and it had not a few Americans muttering, "Oh no, not again!" Yes, another George Bush campaign has begun. Twelve years ago he was shilling for Ronald Reagan as his obsequious running mate. Today, he's the President and wants another term. Not because he has a vision for America — he wants another term because he wants another term, because the President is constitutionally availed two terms.

In 1984, the Reagan/Bush ticket was re-elected. Walter Mondale, the Democratic opponent, made a historic, though very political pick for the second spot on his ticket when he named Congresswoman Geraldine Ferraro. George Bush debated her a week after Reagan squared off against Mondale. Reagan appeared as if he'd just escaped from the Alzheimer's ward of a nursing home. Bush's performance was high-string and goofy, but media pundits nevertheless declared him the winner. The next day, the Vice President, among several macho partisans, talked of "kicking a little ass last night."

By 1988 Bush had risen the political ladder to the point where he was a Presidential candidate. Was this vapid man Presidential material? Columnist George Will called him a "lap dog" for pandering to his most vociferous enemies. Luckily for Bush, his opponent turned out to be a diminutive, ethnic-looking governor with a "funny" surname, Dukakis.

Now another election year is upon us; another one with whining George Bush as a main player. In Bush's first visit to the first primary state, he was in rare form. Rambling and taking potshots at one and all, Bush didn't seem to know who to blame for his woes. The liberals in Congress. Ted Kennedy.

Then there's that troublemaker to the right, Pat Buchanan. "I'm sick and tired of being a punching bag for the lightweights around this country yelling at me day and night. I'm sick of it," the President complained. "I'm sick and tired, I am, every single night I hear one of those carping little liberal Democrats jumping all over my you-know-what."

Well, Mr. Bush, many of us are sick and tired of you. It's bad enough having you as our fearless leader; what's worse is having you as a candidate every four years. Your whining style has played itself out. Only Richard Nixon could top you on the sheer number of national campaigns waged (Nixon was on five national tickets either as a Presidential or Vice-Presidential candidate: '52, '56, '60, '68, and '72).

So we might as well brace ourselves for Bush Campaign #4. And his second with J. Danforth Quayle, one of the few national politicians who makes Bush look Presidential.

It's important that we ask about your health, Mr. President, considering the consequences of your demise or incapacity. Assuring a crowd of New Hampshire Republicans that he was fit as a fiddle, Bush shrieked, "Don't cry for me, Argentina."

It's not Argentina that's crying, Mr. President.

NJN

This is Bush on Drugs

"I'm all for Lawrence Welk. . . Lawrence Welk is a wonderful man. He used to be, or was, wherever he is now, bless him. But you don't need $700,000 for a Lawrence Welk museum when we've got tough times and people in New Hampshire are hurting."

George Bush on the campaign trail, 1992

Maybe George Bush should cancel his next quail-hunting trip, and check into the Betty Ford Clinic. He regularly takes a strong sedative called Halcion, which, according to a chilling op-ed piece in *The New York Times* (written by a Republican), provides a wild trip. It sounds so good I wish I'd tried it during my fogbound years. The article quotes heroin users who say Halcion is an even better high — "It makes the user alternately supremely confident, and then panicky with unamenable dread."

Doesn't sound much different than a weekend

bender. No wonder he threw up in Japan. It wasn't the sushi; *the Prez was stoned!* Just as FDR was "physically challenged" with his polio-withered legs, George Bush is "chemically challenged" by a dangerous hallucinogen that is banned in Britain, and the subject of much litigation and controversy in this country.

The leader of the free world shouldn't be a pill-head. The man with his finger on *The Button* shouldn't be a dope fiend. Bill Clinton's dalliances notwithstanding, he appears to be clean and sober.

Speaking of Clinton, have you ever noticed that Democratic sex scandals are always heterosexual (Barney Frank being the exception), whereas Republican trysts frequently take on a more lurid bent? Congressmen chasing underage boy pages around the Capitol, or right-wing reverends staging orgies that would make Hefner blush.

Clinton's clearly a Democrat in the JFK tradition: a healthy, horny guy, using his power and influence to meet chicks.

Wouldn't you?

JM

Dis Ain't Right

"The liberal vision of a happy, productive and content welfare state hasn't even worked on 22 square miles of the most valuable real estate in the world — one in every eight people [is] on the dole."
Vice President Quayle

The *New York Post* recently ran a headline that "threatened" the Vice President of the United States. "Don't Dis Us," read the message from the "City of New York." It was a retort to critical remarks he made about the city and how it's governed.

The Vice President is a caricature of a golf-playing dunce, with a plasticized pretty face, and a vacuous, robotic personality. The fact that he's a "heartbeat away" is laughable, if one detaches his or herself from the immediate reality.

And the reality for most New Yorkers is that Dan Quayle has stumbled onto the truth for once. The Big Apple is rotting to the core. How many New Yorkers would be willing to wager that things will get better over the next decade? Will the year 2000 be worth celebrating here?

The city is a bureaucratic nightmare. The hoi polloi have little to say in the governing of their town. Voting politicians in and out of office has scant impact on the nuts and bolts minutia of daily living. The poor neighborhoods stay poor, and get poorer. The middle class neighborhoods deteriorate, shrinking day by day, and await the inevitable. Yet, wealthy enclaves proliferate (mainly in Manhattan), seemingly oblivious to the scope of the city's ills.

What's living like for long-time city residents of the

outer boroughs? Last year, for example, NYC at great expense, installed water meters in single and two-family homes. People were just going to have to pay for water used over a certain level. A noble endeavor, and fair enough in this era of shrinking water supplies. But what happened? Homeowners got zapped with exorbitant water bills, double and triple their previous ones, and no city lackey has ever read a meter.

This is just a symptom of the bureaucratic morass, where people get the shaft. What's their recourse? Call a city agency? The bloated mess that runs the city is unresponsive to the constituency it's supposed to serve.

City sanitation troops harass small businesses every day. Ticket books in hand, the walking pencil-pushers strike at will. Mom-and-Pop stores have been slapped with summonses for having a single gum wrapper on their sidewalk. The law requires that they keep their premises clean (great!), but blowing papers, and human depositors, leave their calling cards 24 hours a day.

Translation: If a city goon or goonette wants to write a ticket, he or she can find a ticketee anytime.

If you're poor and living in a poor neighborhood, chances are you're bound to a life of desolation. As for neighborhoods being reborn, just visit Charlotte Street in the South Bronx, where candidates Carter (1976) and Reagan (1980) appeared for a photo-op. Touring the devastation, Carter promised to help. Reagan, four years later, was heckled on the same spot. He shouted back, "I can't do a damn thing for you if I don't get elected." He got elected, and he didn't do a damn thing for them.

No politician or cushy bureaucrat gives a damn. There is no consent of the governed.

NJN

Endangered Feces

There's a Department of Health warning posted at the entrance to a swimming pool I frequent, reading: **URINATION, DISCHARGING OF FECAL MATTER, EXPECTORATION, AND BLOWING OF THE NOSE PROHIBITED IN THE POOL.**

I felt this was a violation of my civil rights. Whenever I'm seized with a wicked urge to discharge fecal matter, my city instinct is to bolt for the nearest public pool.

Were such signs always necessary? Or was there a time, in the elusive "good old days," when there was a social etiquette about such things, an almost innate sense that it was inappropriate to shit in pools?

The New York City Transit Authority has created a "Rules of Conduct" list that is posted at all token booths. Apart from the usual "no smoking," etc., rules, it also includes:

- No destroying subway property.
- No creating an unsanitary condition.
- No lying down.

The New York subway system smells like a dirty toilet, it is defaced and vandalized, and there are many prone souls, blithely snoozing. It seems that the "Rules of Conduct" aren't strictly enforced. I'm curious to know how much the NYCTA spent to print and distribute these posters to every subway station in the five boroughs.

As an act of civil disobedience, I am leaving my keyboard this instant to lie down on a subway platform. And if I'm feeling especially rebellious, I might even discharge some fecal matter.

JM

And The Rest. . .

Twenty-eight years ago, a sitcom called *Gilligan's Island* debuted on CBS with a seven member cast. Some bigwig palooka made a decision that two of the seven actors shouldn't get billing in the opening credits. The beginning theme went like this: *"The ship set down on the shore of this uncharted desert isle with Gilligan, the Skipper too, the Millionaire, and his wife. The Movie Star — and the rest, here on Gilligan's Isle."*

It must have been humiliating for Russell Johnson and Dawn Wells, to be called "the rest," considering their roles were as prominent as any other cast member.

I just got a taste of the "and the rest" stigma.

I recently received literature from the "Jerry Brown for President Committee," asking me if I was interested in becoming a Brown delegate from New York State. I had to first complete a New York State Democratic Party application. A line therein read: "I hereby pledge support to the candidacy of ____________." The Brown people had typed in Edmund G. Brown, Jr.

While I'd love to be a delegate for Brown at the Democratic National Convention in New York this summer, I passed on the opportunity when I learned that I had to gather many signatures from local Democrats to even be considered. Going door-to-door like a vacuum salesman isn't too appealing, particularly in New York City.

That aside, what disturbed me most about the delegate (but hardly delicate) application was the line that read: "I am (check one)." The choices were: African-American, Latino, Native American, and Asian/Pacific American.

Isn't somebody missing here? I would classify myself as a native American, having been born and bred in the Bronx, and never having stepped foot on foreign soil. I don't think that's what the state Democratic hierarchy had in mind when they inquired as to who "I am." There wasn't even an "Other" to check off.

How ridiculous! Some of us are fed up with separating everybody into disparate groups. We're all Americans, isn't that enough?

If 50% of Jerry Brown supporters are black, I hope that number of delegates are represented at the convention for him. But the opportunity goes to every supporter. If Brown's got a large following of Pacific-Americans (a rather new classification), I hope they'll be represented accordingly at the convention.

Prior to 1973, Democratic Conventions were predominantly comprised of white males. This was a travesty, alright — but now the tables have turned to another, equally unhealthy extreme.

The 1988 Democratic Convention was not representative of the Democratic voter nationwide. Far from it. And this appeasement has been killing the party's chances in national elections.

The overt pandering that this application represents is revolting. Toward the bottom, I'm asked how I'm physically challenged, and am asked to list my disability. Inclusion is important, but I don't feel that the Brown delegation needs six people in wheelchairs to make it progressive. And if there weren't a Pacific-American in the lot, would this disqualify Brown from being President?

Please, Democratic mavens, get off this feckless approach. Or at least give me a box to check. "And the rest" just doesn't suit me. How about, "I am an American citizen who wants __________ to be the next President."

NJN

Person Of Colors

Columnist Pete Hamill, in an article about the New Hampshire primary, blasted the entire population of the state as "loathsome lardheads," and "fat, balding white guys wedged into diner booths." He said New Hampshire wasn't representative of Real America because it had no homeless, no Uzi-packing drug czars or crackhouses.

Sounds like a nice place to raise a family, actually.

Not all lardheads are wedged into diner booths. Some are syndicated columnists. Hamill and I are kindred in many ways, but this silly piece is indicative of a scribe who has either lost his edge, or an example of what happens when you have to crank out something to meet a deadline. Which is exactly what I'm doing right now.

Pete, your novella, *The Gift*, a thinly-veiled autobiographical work about your tumultuous relationship with your father, is, in my opinion, a minor masterpiece, and I hope you didn't shoot your creative load with that one.

Your fear of Pat Buchanan becoming a Hitlerian demagogue is unwarranted, and your insinuation that all whites, and only whites, are racist, is pandering pseudo-liberalism at its worst.

"People of color" can hate with the same intensity as so-called "white" folk. I'm classified as a white guy from the Bronx, but I consider myself a person of colors. I'm pink when healthy, pale when sickly, beet-red when boozed-up. My forearms and the backs of my hands are slightly browned by the sun, and the head of my penis is lavender in romantic candlelight. I am, in fact, a creature of many tints and hue

So let's stop all this nonsense and love one another baby. Even the fat, balding lardheads wedged into diner booths.

JM

Nightmare on 161st Street

Directly behind *The House That Ruth Built*, Yankee Stadium, lies an equally imposing edifice. A place where justice is meted out on a daily basis. Or so we'd like to believe. If you're a Bronx resident past school age, you're supposed to be called to serve on jury duty every two years (though the same people seem to be summoned all the time, while others avoid it their whole lives).

I don't know what it's like to serve on jury duty in smaller population centers, or more affluent ones, but doing one's duty in the Bronx is seldom a lot of laughs.

It's not all a grind. It's interesting to observe up close how our justice system works. But when it takes three days to select a jury for a simple burglary case. . .

Last month, while serving my tour on 161st Street, I was on a panel of prospective jurors being questioned by a lawyer and a judge. The crime was murder. The accused, who had a translator pumping Spanish into his ear throughout the proceedings, sat stonily in the backdrop. The murder, that may or may not have been committed by the accused, occurred in October of 1989. That's two and a half years ago.

Fourteen at a time, we filled the jury box and were grilled by the judge, an assistant district attorney, and the defense attorney. What did we do for a living, did we know any law enforcement people, and could we be just plain ol' fair, were just a few queries hurled at us anxiety-ridden Bronxites. This particular courtroom was large, and the acoustics were lousy. An aged stenographer, way past her prime, scowled and muttered, "I can't hear you. What? I can't hear you." The attorney for the accused was a lumbering Raymond Burr (circa 1992) type, who needed a cane to steady himself. Not because he was old, but because he was horribly overweight, gasping for every breath. He implored us not to pre-judge his client because he couldn't speak English. "Does that make him guilty?"

After the judge's required spiel and the questioning was complete, the legal teams huddled in The Robe's chambers for 10 minutes. When they solemnly emerged, a clerk (usually the dumbest of hack bureaucrats) read the names of those who should remain. As I was being ushered out I saw that only three people had made the cut. The whole process had taken three hours.

It was back to the jury room again to listen for my name again, and my next assignment. I didn't have to wait too long. In 15 minutes, I was off to another courtroom and another case. This one: armed robbery. This time the accused could apparently comprehend English; he had no translator. I don't know if he would be classified as a black man or a Latino. His hair was shaved on the sides (it's called a "fade" — Hitler had one), and he wore an earring. This courtroom was not a Perry Mason set like the previous one. It was more of a storage closet converted into a justice center. The accused had his girlfriend or wife in the little gallery for spectators. She held a small child and wore a nose-ring. One potential juror, when asked what she liked to do in her spare time, answered, "Shop." The judge and lawyers laughed. Parenthetically, she added that she had "champagne tastes and beer money."

This time, four of the fourteen questioned were tapped to serve. The lady with champagne tastes was among them. I was not, and was not unhappy. Being sequestered with the champagne lady was a nightmarish prospect.

Back to the jury room to be dismissed for the day.

"We'll see you all on Monday," was the parting shot from a well-paid bureaucrat.

Monday brought with it a new herd of disgruntled citizens called to do their civic duty. Some of the tired old bunch, who started on Thursday, or the previous Monday, would likely get the good word: Good-bye! I was mercifully let go after only three days of "service." Two years ago, almost to the day, I was actually selected to sit in a jury and sit in judgment on an alleged drug dealer. His peers found him not guilty — he's probably back in business. Two years before that, I was held for nine days and never selected to sit on a jury.

If you're in a hurry, don't commit a crime in the Bronx.

NJN

Cry Havoc, and Let Slip the Dogs of War

Part of a gentleman's code includes not kicking a fella when he's down. The videotape evidence of the LA cops clubbing Rodney King into insensibility clearly shows excessive force at its worst. They had him where they wanted him; there was no need for the continued pummeling. It would seem that the jury system has failed once again.

This does not, however, give rabble-rousers and agitators just cause to run riot and tear up the town. Innocent people being pulled from their cars and beaten to death, homes being torched, and other assorted mayhem are not acts of justice. This is brutal conduct that can't be condoned.

I'm a 30-year-old white male who has never owned a slave. I have never oppressed anyone. In fact, my ancestors suffered centuries of tyranny, torture, and terrorism at the bloody hands of the British Empire, but I wouldn't attack John Cleese or Michael Caine if I met them on the street. I wouldn't demand reparations from them; I don't think they owe me anything.

Many paternalistic, pandering pseudo-liberals who love minorities (as long as they don't live next door), and who are afraid to ride the subways, smugly "understood" the LA riots (from a discreet distance). It wasn't their shattered skull that oozed blood on the asphalt, savagely beaten by a black lynch mob because their pigmentation is similar to the cops who clobbered Rodney King.

I ride the New York City subway system daily, and am routinely jostled, challenged and stared down by young black men. They know nothing about me, yet they take an instant dislike to me. Because I wear a fashionable blazer/slacks combo and cheap tie, they think I'm Yuppie scum, their tormentor, ***The Man***. If they saw my bottom line, they'd realize I was a member of the working poor, not doing much better than an unskilled laborer. Yet they regard me with hateful resentment, simply because my skin color is different than their own. *That's racism!* I can't abide racism in any form, and I resent the fact the selective racism is accepted and unchallenged by politicians and the media.

A local morning news program did a live remote from a predominantly Irish-American Bronx neighborhood recently, and the anchor in the studio (a babe of color, by the way) made a racist joke to the reporter at the scene. To paraphrase: "You can tell it's an Irish neighborhood. Look at all the bars." Imagine if a white reporter had similarly slurred a black, Hispanic or Asian neighborhood.

He would have been summarily dismissed and probably blacklisted.

There's a disturbing double-standard here, that is, in the long run, mere lip service from the powers-that-be. It's to their advantage to keep tensions high among the underclass. With interracial skull-cracking fast becoming America's favorite pastime, no unity, hence no change will ever happen. The fatcats and bigwigs continue to look down from Mount Olympus, and laugh all the way to the bank.

JM

The "Ought Not to Be" Mayor

There's a New York City public affairs station (WNYC) that shows Mayor Dinkins's daily meetings with the local press. Politician-press encounters, depending on who's the pol, can be entertaining spectacles. Richard Nixon told America that he wasn't a crook during one (he was), Gary Hart denied that he ever committed adultery (he did), and a Pennsylvania Attorney General blew his brains out after declaring his innocence in a breaking scandal (he was guilty).

But Mayor David Dinkins rarely has anything titillating or useful to offer the voracious city scribes. He's an absolutely humorless stiff, and an uninspiring bore who's a poor excuse for the leader of the country's most populous metropolis.

Dinkins is, however, a rather skilled tennis player. It's his favorite pastime, and, seemingly, his only emotional outlet. When questioned recently about his personal use of a public tennis facility, the Mayor testily bristled at the folly of such press fishing expeditions. It was a joke story, so why didn't the Mayor treat it as such? The tennis affair cried out for levity. It cried out for Dinkins to make light of the whole thing.

But, no! David Dinkins has no sense of humor, least of all about himself. He's even made his clown prince of a predecessor, Ed Koch, seem appealing. Koch, for all his selling out to wealthy real estate interests, was at least an amusing performer at times, who could spar with the best of them on any subject. Why then, is this fellow Dinkins the mayor of the most renowned city in the world?

He's black. That was and is the only reason he was elected. And he hides behind his skin color. Legitimate criticism of his listless leadership is called racist by many in his inner-circle, and many on the outside, too. And this woeful clamor is growing tiresome.

Dinkins beat out Ed Koch, Richard Ravitch, and Harrison Goldin in the last mayoral primary. Koch had worn out his welcome, and the other more intelligent alternatives weren't given a chance by the media, who decreed that it was Koch versus the Black man — *Period.* Dinkins was virtually assured of the entire black vote because it was time for the city to have a black mayor.

It didn't matter that he was a most ordinary politician, and that's the best one could say about Dinkins's qualifications. A consummate hack would be more accurate. His record is blandly uninspiring. Still, he beat Koch and squared-off against Republican Rudolph Giuliani in the November election.

Giuliani, as a successful federal prosecutor, had a genuine issue to run on — Clean Government. The city's political structure had just been wracked by major scandal, with many powerful and visible public officials going to jail. One even killed himself. This was all lost in the whirl of racial politics. Dinkins promised that his presence in Gracie Mansion would lessen the tensions so widespread in the city. He proclaimed himself a "healer." The press bought this image of Dinkins as Mr. Nice Guy, a true conciliator and quite a contrast to the big-mouthed, antagonistic Ed Koch.

A possible Giuliani victory was seen as tantamount to admitting that The Big Apple was a haven for bigots and haters. David Dinkins could not be rejected on the basis of his character. He didn't, among other things, file income tax returns for four years in the early 1970's, claiming he was too busy or simply forgot. There was an implicit threat by some of his more militant supporters: *Elect Dinkins or watch the city burn.*

David Dinkins won by a hair. It's now fair to conclude that he has been no Jesus Christ on matters of healing. Racial strife is worse than ever, and the empty (but expensive) suited mayor seems at a loss for solutions.

It's hardly racist to criticize Dinkins or any other black elected official. It's racist to pull punches and treat a "person of color" differently, as many do. Many, in fact, on the patronizing political left.

Dinkins is mayor. His two years in office have been rudderless, very much like the three-year reign of George Bush in Washington. Both men ought to be retired as soon as possible. Bush could hunt quail from dawn to dusk, and Dinkins could play tennis to his heart's desire.

NJN

Pederasts On Parade

Last year, New York's gay community made quite a fuss at the St. Patrick's Day parade. There was a grand donnybrook over whether they should march at all. They finally did, with the blessing of Mayor Dinkins, and the outrage of many others. Throw a stick in this town and you won't hit many liberal Irish or Irish-Americans. Unless, of course, you're aiming at me. And even I regard the *Lavender Hill Mob's* motives with suspicion.

I don't think the militant laddies were genuinely interested in banding together to celebrate their Celtic heritage. Rest assured, the homosexual population has doubtlessly been well-represented in the parade since its inception. In my opinion, they just used it as an excuse to rile their arch-nemesis, John Cardinal O'Connor, since the parade route passes right by his humble abode, St. Patrick's Cathedral. Literally and figuratively mooning Johnny the Card is not the worst hobby one can have. I've taken more than my share of potshots at him. This was, however, before the emergence of the more serene and humble Mannion of late.

There are a constellation of soul-components that make us what we are, and sexual orientation is but one aspect of our complex personae. I'll be working this St. Patrick's Day, otherwise I might march with the county of my forbears. And if there was a group of Irishmen that marched under the banner *"Micks Into S&M Scenarios With Spandex-Clad Scandinavian Stewardesses,"* I might feel compelled to join them. I would proudly strut up Fifth Avenue with them, and there'd be a tear in my eye as I sang in my best castrati-falsetto, *"Ireland must be heaven, 'cause me mother came from there."*

JM

Hi, Honey. . . I'm Sick

"You know something? If you couldn't read, you couldn't look up what was on television."
Beaver Cleaver

A local television station recently ran a program which purported to look at the impact of the boob tube over five decades. A survey was cited that said the average American watched seven hours of TV a day. The show seemed grounded in the opinion that today's programming is more realistic and societally valuable than their 1950's and 1960's cousins.

Teenagers were interviewed, as were their parents. The youths praised shows like *Beverly Hills 90210*, applauding its hipness and issues-of-the-day orientation. One parent lamented the fact that families sitting down at the dinner table, or just talking, was absent from today's TV menu. He said the dinner scenes were positive, and he approved of *Leave It To Beaver*, *Father Knows Best*, and *The Donna Reed Show*.

I confess to being a nostalgic television buff, and no fan of the current line-up. I've never watched *Beverly Hills 90210*, but I do watch *The Beverly Hillbillies*. I've never seen an episode of *Doogie Howser* or the now-infamous *Murphy Brown*. I prefer selection from television's "lurid" past: *The Andy Griffith Show*, *The Twilight Zone*, *The Fugitive*, etc. Non-news TV is an escape from the grind of reality. I can't then be critical of the "unrealistic" programming of days gone by.

The sitcoms of today take credit for dealing with serious matters: unwanted pregnancies, drugs, and a host of societal maladies. What I see are ridiculously phony sets, cheap laughs and stilted acting. Conveying a sense of reality is the last thing these shows accomplish.

I wonder if we're so better off with today's programming than we were with the popular '60's westerns. True, we were never told how many women Little Joe Cartwright impregnated, or if ol' Hoss was really gay, or that Ben, the patriarch, was an abusive, alcoholic father.

I like vicariously visiting The Ponderosa. I like the slow pace of Mayberry, North Carolina. I even get a kick out of *Dragnet*, with Jack Webb's corny moralizing. I feel that if Joe Friday was still with the LAPD, we wouldn't have had last year's incendiary riots. I don't see us as a psychologically better off culture thanks to the "liberation" of television.

The shows of the past conveyed a sense of simplicity. A simplicity that has now been trampled upon by technological advancement and the population explosion. David Jannsen traversed America as a fugitive from justice, hopping freights and riding buses. America loomed larger and more remote. There were no *Unsolved Mysteries* and *America's Most Wanted* shows to aid in the capture of fugitives by displaying computer enhanced pictures for millions of viewers.

Television reflects the times. Surely, the more repressed era of the '50's and '60's gave us fantasy families. Yet *Married. . . With Children*, and *Roseanne*, are fantasy families on the opposite end of the spectrum. The diseased minds who policed programming three decades ago have produced the diseased minds of today who give us contemporary garbage and claim a higher brand.

NJN

1991

I stopped drinking in November of 1990, and NJN got less didactic, so 1991 was a year of healing for both of us. Political punditry took a back seat to wide-ranging social commentary and fluff pieces designed to provoke and amuse. We had given up (for the most part) trying to preach. A man is truly wise when he admits he really knows nothing, which makes my colleague and I truly wise guys.

Drunken Poets Society

In an earlier issue of this journal of opinion, an article appeared entitled "Designer Dependency," about how it is fashionable for Hollywood phonies to enter recovery programs (most of which have the word "anonymous" in their names), then announce it to the world on national television. If you read it and felt that Mannion was not in top form, there's a reason — I didn't write it. I was too loaded to turn out a single page (double-spaced) at the time. The editor wrote it, attached my name, and you, dear reader, were none the wiser.

Ouch!

I write my own stuff these days, and still have a few thoughts on the subject. I met an old acquaintance on the street the other day, a fellow saloonatic whom I hadn't seen in months. He was clear-eyed and trim; not the bloated, moonfaced madman of half a year ago.

"Did you hear that Ally Sheedy wrote a book of recovery-themed poetry?" he inquired.

I said I had.

Have you read it?"

"No."

"I thought you were her biggest fan. She made you swoon."

"I wasn't swooning, I was staggering."

"How's that?"

"I've seen most of her movies, and she has starred in several kinky fantasies of mine, but she has never inspired me to shoot the President."

"You should read it and review it in your newsletter."

"That would be unwise."

"How's that?"

"I might be acerbic."

"You're good at that."

"Yes, but our eyes might meet across a crowded room one day, and a bad review might ruin my chances with her."

"That's a rather slim possibility."

"I believe in miracles."

"So do I. Now."

"How did you arrive at this attitude adjustment?

"As you may have noticed, I was going nowhere mighty fast. One afternoon I was drinking a Heineken on a park bench in Manhattan, trying to take the edge off a wicked hangover, and Judd Nelson walked by. Y'know, the actor?"

"The guy who emotes by flaring his nostrils."

"Yeah! Anyway, I saw him strutting by, no suit and tie, in no hurry. Looking contented as hell. Suddenly I had a moment of clarity. I thought to myself — if this guy can achieve the degree of success he has in his profession, than I certainly can in mine, if I give up my destructive habits and turn my life around. I finished that Heineken and haven't had a drink since. And every night

I thank Judd Nelson for helping me stay sober one day at a time."

We shook hands and parted. A few days later I received a copy of Miss Sheedy's book in the mail, along with a collection of poems written by my friend. He wanted me to sample Ally's verse and compare it with his own, and possibly print a few of his in this newsletter. He believed that Ally's verse was published on her name recognition factor alone, and that he, a lesser known poet, would appreciate this forum to express himself.

Their poetry is thematically similar. Miss Sheedy, in an ode to junk food subtitled "I Am Not A Corn Chip," ends on the life-affirming note, "*I am not a corn chip/I tell her/And I'm not.*"

This is suspiciously similar to my friend's melancholic dirge, "I Am Not A Hip Flask."

"*I am not a hip flask/Need you even ask?/'Tis a terrible task/To be snug 'gainst the ass/Of an alcoholic bum/I'm emotionally numb!!!*"

This unrelenting shriek of agonizing fury is followed by the sequel, "I Am Not a 25 Ounce Can Of Foster's Lager, Either!"

Ms. Sheedy writes candidly of her hospitalization in "There's Been a Slight Mistake — Rehab 3 a.m." wherein she speaks of denial: "*I DON'T HAVE A PROBLEM/It's all a slight mistake, nurse-Bitch/(God, I'm hot.)/I've never had any kind of problem — Demi, you little witch.*"

Equally traumatic is my friend's poem, simply called "Beer."

"*So what, I drink beer/What are you, a queer?/Spare me your leer/Your impertinent sneer/Real Men drink beer/My dear!*"

With all due respect, I think these formerly drunken poets should get about the business of getting better anonymously, in the company of kindred souls who've shared the pain and can help the healing process. No one else can really understand, and what makes these poets think that anyone else really cares? Pain is not automatically art. Sometimes pain is just pain.

As arts & entertainment editor of *The Progressive Pragmatist*, I would be remiss not to offer a formal review of Ally Sheedy's book of poetry, *Yesterday I Saw The Sun*: Ally Sheedy is a pretty woman and gifted actress, and I eagerly await her next movie.

As for me, I used to be a member of the Drunken Poet's Society, but I don't write poetry anymore.

And that has made all the difference.

JM

The opposite is the case. I actually stopped drinking and started writing poetry, to equal doses of acclaim and infamy, I might add. While I'm confessing, I might as well admit that the whole article is bogus. I made the whole thing up. So much for my journalistic integrity.

***There, I feel much better.
Thank you for letting me share.***

NJN followed my lead and tried his hand at dialogue-laden, faux-reportage with this next piece. I doubt this conversation ever took place, but what the hell. . .

The Faith's Pretender

"Hey, Ralph, you going to read the new book about Nancy Reagan?"

"I wouldn't read that trash for all the spaghetti in Little Italy. I hope you don't believe that garbage, Eric. Nancy Reagan is a great lady. What about them stinkin' Kennedys? Kills a woman and gets away with it. I bet his nephew gets off, too."

"At least the Kennedys help working stiffs from time to time. Reagan and the Mrs. never gave a hoot about Regular Joes like you and me."

"What are you talking about? He cut the government down to size, and tried to stop liberals like Kennedy from giving our money to lazy bums on welfare."

"How do you explain the big budget deficits? If Nancy hadn't bought all those expensive red dresses, the government would probably be in the black."

"So she wanted to look good. All women are vain. Nancy, she was representin' this country. She wasn't like the old dames in this neighborhood, runnin' around with orange and blue hair. Eric, I want the White House to look good, and I want it painted, too."

"But the Reagans tried to pass themselves off as church-goers. Y'know, good Christians. They just didn't hit the mark, not by a longshot."

"Reagan said they didn't want to inconvenience the other worshippers by showin' up with the Secret Service. And I believe him."

"You wanna buy a bridge, Ralph? Forget church, look at his kids. They're all screwed up. The daughter's book makes 'em out to be pretty lousy parents."

"Who are you, God Almighty? Do not judge, least you be judged, pal. That's what the Bible says."

"Ralph, answer me this — would you want Nancy Reagan to be your mother?"

"You leave my mother out of this, God rest her soul."

"Would you want her as your sister? Your wife?"

"I'd trade my Babs any day for Nancy."

"Nancy was fast and loose in her prime, Ralph. You think you could've handled her?"

"You kiddin'? That's one thing Ted Kennedy and I have in common."

"What's that?"

"We both got a hunger that's hard to satisfy. But don't get me wrong. I believe in the sanctity of the marriage vow. Once you say, 'I do,' the fun's over."

"You think Reagan fooled around. The book says he seduced a teenager when he was governor."

"He's not the type. Kennedys do that."

"Come on, Ralphie, the Reagans are frauds."

"Frauds nothin'. The Kennedys have done a lot worse things than the Reagans."

Okay, Ralphie. How about this — all rich people, Reagans, Kennedys, whoever, play by a different set of rules. Our laws don't apply to them."

"Right. Rich people stink!"

"Including the Reagans."

"Yeah."

You're learnin', Ralphie boy."

NJN

Okay, so it's not a Socratic dialogue, but you get the point. HYPOCRISY ALERT: NJN trashed Kitty Kelley during the run of The Progressive Pragmatist, but borrows liberally from her book about Nancy to trash the Reagans. Hmmm. . .

More philosophizing, this time from yours truly. This is an example of starting with a great title and dashing off a piece to go underneath it. Again, the dialogue that opens the essay never took place. Our literary license knew no bounds.

Of Mouse and Mannion

"Hey, Sal. I've got a new pet."

"Don't let it shit in da courtyard."

"I didn't adopt him, Sal. He squeezed through a crack in the wall."

"A mouse?"

"Yeah."

"Dis is da Bronx. Be glad it's not a rat."

Boiler-room philosophy from my superintendent. The same guy who doesn't give his tenants hot water in the summer, reasoning, "It's hot. Whatcha need hot water for?"

No matter how clean you keep an apartment in a prewar tenement in the Bronx, one must contend with vermin. Whether they're roaches in the bathroom, or ghetto-blasting punks on the corner, the quality of life in NYC has gone to hell. Smug Governor Cuomo sings his own praises, and urbane but irascible Mayor Dinkins testily bristles at the suggestion that all is not well, but reality is reality. Taxes rise, the infrastructure crumbles, and mice have invaded apartment 3B.

I tried humanitarian traps. I tried guillotine traps. I finally had to resort to those gruesome glue traps. An awful way to go, but his presence was a violation of my inner sanctum. And his chewing up my books and papers indicated that he was a she, and was building a nest.

She was a cagey creature. Wise to glue traps, she simply pushed them aside and scurried past them. I was developing a grudging respect for the rodent, but I had to discover her lair before I had a family of furballs disturbing my domestic tranquillity.

I finally tore my room apart, and, upon moving a bookcase that hadn't been moved in 20 years, discovered a nest of dust, paper, and string. She bolted before I pummeled the mass with a crutch, slaughtering four young ones.

I cleaned the bloody mess, and was putting my room back in order. When moving a pillow, the mother leapt out of the pillowcase. My reaction was not unlike the stereotype of a woman who leaps upon a chair and screams, "Eeek." Regaining my composure, I chased it around the room, and in its careless frenzy, it landed on a glue trap. The Great White Hunter had its prey. We looked into each other's eyes and I saw fear, maybe even a little sadness. I mercifully bashed it with my crutch. Bright red blood splattered, her hind legs twitched for a few seconds, and she was gone.

I guess I'm a nice guy after all, for I felt terrible afterward. Even as I write this, my skin crawls. I nervously jump at every squeak of the wooden floors, every unfamiliar noise within the walls. She is not alone.

When I saw the mouse on the glue trap, I realized that life is like a glue trap for many people. They feel paralyzed. They whine about their lot, wriggle and twitch in impotent defiance, squeal and squeak in protest, and eventually *the big stick* descends with a crunch, ending their misery.

Unlike the unfortunate mouse, our glue traps are of our own making. I recently and reluctantly crawled off mine. Controlling your own destiny is frightening at times, but mandatory if you're going to achieve success and serenity in this world. It's a risk worth taking, because a life of quiet desperation really sucks! The glue trap will always be there, in the darkest corner of your soul. You're free to step back on anytime.

Submitted for your approval — a half-baked parable out of a mundane episode in the mad realm of urban decay.

JM

NJN gets nostalgic in the next piece, immortalizing a former schoolmate of both of us, with uncharacteristic warmth.

May The Farce Be With You

All of us have gone to school with someone truly unique, someone who stood out from the others like a proverbial sore thumb. Or, in my old friend Julio's case, a sore "jhzu-jhzu-jhzu finger."

In my grammar school, there was this kid named Julio. He was of Cuban descent. In those days (the mid-'70's) Julio was part of the minority. The school had a smattering of blacks and Hispanics, but racial distinctions were not a factor in forming friendships.

People got along or didn't based on personality. Julio

was a friend to any and all who appreciated his unorthodox antics. He would swear in Spanish. On any given day, he'd "boon-yetta" you to death with fits of real or affected anger. That's a phonetic spelling, but he was saying "damn," or some equivalent. He also called many of his peers "bingas." I later learned that little Julio was referring to his pee-wee brethren as a part of the male anatomy.

But there was more to Julio than uttering slang in a high-pitched foreign tongue. Julio was a product of the Sexual Revolution of the 1960's and '70's. He held nothing back.

Julio pinched his peers. He'd sneak up on unsuspecting boys, stick his finger in their stomachs, wiggle it a bit, mimicking the sound of a drill. "Jzhu-jzhu-jzhu," he'd giggle in youthful triumph.

Julio, I later learned, was more than a pincher. He was a poet and child satirist. When we were parting ways to attend different high schools, out came the autograph albums and yearbooks to sign. This activity separated the Julios from the foolios.

There were four categories of signees. The "good luck in high school" people. Boring, but all-purpose. There were the kids who consulted books of catch-phrases like, "In your ocean of friends, count me as a permanent wave." Anyone who wrote that was not likely a friend at all. And there was the flip side of this, those who transcribed the hackneyed phrases we probably thought were pretty funny at the time: *"When you get married and live in a tree/Send me a coconut C.O.D."*

Lastly, there were the originals. And Julio was an original. Contributing Editor and former schoolmate James Mannion, is fortunate to have in his possession two Julio-penned gems.

The Cuban-American sage signed his picture in

Mannion's yearbook: *"To Ugly — have a bad time in high school."* In Mannion's autograph album, Julio inscribed this poem: *"Roses are Red/Violets are Blue/I hate you/You blowhorn."*

A genius! Where have you gone, Julio? Hopefully, you haven't "jzhu-jzhu-jzhued" the wrong person and gotten yourself in trouble. Yes, Julio, you're looking more and more like a comic genius with each passing year.

One last ode to you, wherever you are, and may the farce be with you. *"To Ugly: Hope you're having a good time in life, but please remove the curse you placed on James Mannion. He did have a bad time in high school, and he's not sure the hex expired upon graduation."*

NJN

And I'm not ugly, by the way.

Here's another personal piece of mine, which, rather than designed to follow a clever title, was composed to precede a droll punch line.

This Gentleman's Head

I like to go to movies on weekday afternoons, when there are only a handful of people in the theater. I don't go to talk to the person I'm with, or to listen to others talk. In a Manhattan multiplex recently, I settled into a seat to watch Mel Brooks' *Life Stinks* (so did the movie, by the way). I practically had the theater to myself. My pleasant isolation was interrupted by a couple of old bags, who, with an entire auditorium of seats to choose from, elected to sit directly behind me.

"Can you see beyond this gentleman's head?" asked

one.

"I can see. He's not that tall," said the other.

Then they launched into a loud dialogue about shopping and grandchildren as the opening credits rolled. I changed my seat.

A few days later, in Hyannis, Mass., taking in a live performance of Don Rickles, I found myself seated in front of two New England WASPs, stock characters out of a short story by Johns Cheever or Updike. Soft middle-aged preppies, who began to complain, though masking it behind falsely amiable kidding, that my head was obstructing their view. I should have told the yokels to cut the conviviality crap. "You're scumbags," I wish I'd said. "You know it, I know it. Just try and be the best scumbags you can."

I'm not a six-footer, nor is my cranium particularly over-sized. I can only assume that my charismatic, larger than life presence creates the illusion that my head is bigger than it actually is. An illusion, which, I hope, extends to other body parts.

JM

Was the set-up worth the pay-off? I think so.

Here's some unabashed sexism, based to some extent on insecurity, and to a large degree on the reverse-sexism I experienced as a male secretary in a major publishing house. I'm President of my own publishing company now, and the only one around to harass or be harassed by is NJN. Hence, I assure you, we are a chaste operation.

Let's Make Love

When women are asked to list men's desirable qualities in surveys, "eyes," and a "sense of humor" invariably top the list. I've been told I have beautiful baby blues, clear and sparkling windows to the soul; no longer the lifeless bloodshot slits of my fogbound years. And, in my humble estimation, I can make 'em laugh.

The women at my job obviously never responded to these surveys, for they neither have nor enjoy a sense of humor. I read an article in the paper about how men still reign supreme in corporate America, and I cut out the headline **(MEN STILL RULE IN THE OFFICE)** and taped it to the entrance of my minuscule cubicle. After several stares of icy silence, the senior Vice President (a man) came by and asked me to remove it. He did so affably, jocularly commenting that "the ladies were offended."

"Not politically correct, eh?" I observed, and we laughed at the thin, yet eminently strokable skins of those tight-assed business gals.

The skirts just didn't get it. I'm no bigwig in the company. I'm an underpaid, overtaxed, embattled White Male. Therein lies the irony of placing such a sign in my cubicle. I'm just a low-level paper-pusher who spends most of his time trying to *look* busy.

A word to the distaffers: If all you want is polite lip service in this *Age of the Euphemism*, the powers-that-be will gladly give it, but this she-fascist jazz will get you nowhere.

It's also a real turn-off. Let's put an end to this war of the sexes. Let's appreciate our differences, lighten up and have some fun. Let's undulate between the sheets in a celebratory horizontal dance of life, love, and equality.

JM

NJN now fondly recalls his collegiate years, and tries to make a few salient points along the way.

He's An Egyptian, By The Way

To help educate me some seven years ago, my esteemed *alma mater*, Manhattan College in the Bronx, briefly gave me the services of a unique professor for a few short weeks. He was a substitute adjunct professor of economics: a tall gawky, swarthy Egyptian gentleman who wore high-water pants and what appeared to be size 20 shoes. He carried a worn out satchel with a buckle on it, and wrote on the blackboard with a rainbow of colored chalks. The macroeconomics graphs looked magnificent, if nothing else. However, he never understood that most students didn't carry five-color pens in their pockets.

"Dr. Z" was the most enthusiastic professor I ever had, even if I couldn't comprehend what he was saying most of the time. He roared out his lectures in not-so-perfect English. "There is no P as in Peter and B as in Ball in Arabic," he informed us, so he always made a "mish-mesh of the two." I suppose it's safe to say that there is no Arab walking the desert named Peter Ball.

Dr. Z filled in for a young woman professor who was having "back problems." She might well have been recovering from some chemical dependency, if her unpredictable classroom behavior was any indication. She looked stoned on more than one occasion.

In any event, fate moved its huge hand and Dr. Z materialized. He implored us to please sign the attendance sheet lest he lose his job. He desperately needed the money, he said. After he lectured us for 55 minutes, he was off to Brooklyn Community College for another fill-in assignment. A few subway transfers in an unfamiliar city. "I live between the muggers and the hippies," he told us. Where exactly that was, we never asked.

Somewhere in the education of Dr. Z, when he was learning English, one of his mentors must have used the expression "by the way." "This is our last meeting, by the way. I'd like to thank each and every one of you, by the way," he said on his final day with us. And so it was. I never heard of the misadventures of Dr. Z again. He was truly dedicated.

* * *

In 1984, Dr. Z commented on the Democratic Presidential primaries. He said he was impressed with George McGovern above the others because McGovern seemed to recognize that it's a question of the "have-nots versus the haves" in world affairs, as well as on the domestic front.

Dr. Z, born and raised in impoverished, over-populated Egypt, was in tune with the lower classes' cry that the world economic pie be more equitably distributed.

It would be nice if that were the case, by the way.

NJN

NJN now takes on the baseball industry, three years before the infamous 1994 strike that has pretty much soured the populace on the once-noble national pastime.

Hey, Hot Dogs!

Attending a professional baseball game ain't what it used to be, and you don't have to be an old timer to say that. Baseball is big business and you're reminded of it every time you enter a stadium.

Forty years ago, in many of the now-bulldozed parks, advertisements adorned the outfield walls. Beer and cigarette ads were omnipresent, and the players were at the mercy of autocratic owners.

Today, players are no longer slaves to the owners. It's the greedy players who get most of the negative press, while owners cry the blues about not being able to pay the bills and turn a profit.

Watching a Mets game live at Shea Stadium is still an exciting experience for me personally, and particularly for idealistic youths who haven't been spoiled by the sport's money spin.

Granted, taking a youngster to a live event is risky business. Galoots abound and ball games are magnets for these blowhards. It's a place for many a joker to let off steam. Unfortunately, much of their hot air is profanity-laden, beer-scented, and just plain stupid.

Notwithstanding the crass money aspect of Major League Baseball and the presence of society's boobs at these games, baseball is still the sport it always has been (at least in the National League, which has no DH, and is still strategically pure). It's still America's pastime.

You walk into a ballpark and smell hot dogs, and a host of aromas that blend with the sound of bat meeting ball. There's a buzz in baseball crowds that isn't matched in other sports.

"Baseball is boring," some argue. Perhaps boring

people find it so. Pay three bucks for a frank, it's worth it. The late Humphrey Bogart said in a public service announcement for the game: "A hot dog in the ballpark beats roast beef at The Ritz."

Indeed it does.

NJN

The Archbishop of New York was not spared criticism in 1991, but he asked for it with this hilarious bit of medieval theologizing.

Quote The Raving: *"God is a Man."*

This was the headline of the *New York Post*, Monday, June 17, 1991. It paraphrases John Cardinal O'Connor, pontificating from his pulpit the day before, pronouncing with certainty the maleness of The Creator. He was responding to equally obnoxious radical feminists; those malevolent she-fascists who are as monomanically mundane as Johnny The Card & Co.

If you're a regular reader of this rag, you know Condom O'Connor has been the inspiration of mucho heresy on my part. The kinder, gentler, serene and humble Mannion of the last few months has not mentioned his formerly favorite target, this flowing fountain of pomposity, this titanic blowhard. I've been waiting for him to make the next move. Thank you, Eminent Johnny, for giving me the excuse to offer you and yours a little religious instruction.

God *(as I understand Him)* is a spiritual entity, a noncorporeal life-force. To argue about whether this incomprehensible source of Light and Life has testicles is to insult The Creator, creating It in our image.

Christ was a product of a patriarchal society, hence his language and symbolism are male-based. If Christ comes again He may very well be a She. Certainly some of the apostles would be. She'd be a member of the lower class, a "minority" (the majority in my neighborhood these days), and the Last Supper might be held at the local McDonald's, with Quarter Pounders, fries and Cokes for all. Maybe Judas would opt for McNuggets.

The pettiness and ignorance of humanity is evident in this dumb and offensive debate between an intractable, cranky old fart and a crew of shrewish, asexual dames. I'm sure The Almighty's advice would be similar to my own: Go out and get laid, you maniacs. Undulate those hips, boys and girls. You won't give a damn about God's genitals if you keep yours healthy and happy.

JM

NJN also dealt with the religious issues in another "Quote The Raving" segment.

Quote The Raving:
"Booga, booga. . .ahhh! I'm going to kill you. . .aah!"

In one of the most bizarre visuals in recent television, ABC's *20/20*, filmed a Catholic priest exorcising a young girl.

In theatrical fashion, the diagnosed psychotic shifted from infantile calm to frothing rage without missing a beat.

This, we were asked to consider, was Satan mouthing off through an innocent child. The demonic duo within her, identifying themselves as "minga" and "zion" cried out in menacing tones, "I'm going to kill you." But most of the time they were incoherent, babbling "booga. . .booga," and the like.

The ritual, performed for a mass audience and sanctioned by some in the Catholic Church hierarchy, made for titillating viewing, but what did they seek to gain by making an exorcism a media spectacle?

Did the Church really believe that this sideshow would convince disenfranchised skeptics that it was in fact blessed with powers from above? If this was the goal, they failed.

All that *20/20* revealed in this segment was that some people are mentally ill. New York City Mayor David Dinkins promised to put a cop on every subway train. He hasn't kept that promise. Surprise! On just about every subway train is a raving madman or madwoman. If "Gina" (the girl on *20/20*) was possessed by Satan, then those deranged straphangers certainly are. They similarly spew incoherence in a cacophony of voices that would make Rich Little envious.

There are more things in heaven and earth, Horatio. . . Still, the notion of Lucifer and his offspring globe-trotting the planet and planting themselves in little girls is somewhat farfetched. What's the Devil's strategy? Why not possess some higher-profile individuals and make some real waves? Come to think of it, maybe he has.

Satan can take heart in the latest Gallup poll which shows that 55% of the respondents believe in him and 49% believe he's capable of possessing their neighbors.

Obviously, there are a few of God's children who have gone awry, who are bad through and through and incapable of redemption. But Superman can take Batman — no contest. So why doesn't God just beat the Red Devil over the head with his own pitchfork? Then maybe we could all live happily ever after.

NJN

Being basically apolitical, I was loath to write political pieces, but I tried on occasion. Here are two short pieces, where a famous Republican and a famous Democrat are treated with equal disrespect.

An Ass By Any Other Name

George Bush, in a calculated leak to prove he's a tough guy, used the word "ass." In a closed door meeting with several congressmen, he assured them that, in the event of a war, Saddam Hussein would "get his ass kicked." This made the headlines of the more scurrilous rags and was the top story on the sleaziest news broadcasts. It's a sound byte meant to inspire meatheads to give each other high fives.

Bush has done it before. After debating Geraldine Ferraro in 1984, he boasted how he "kicked a little ass." Only Mr. and Mrs. Zaccaro know the true size of her ass, but Bush was standing nearby, and he checked out what he perceived to be a little one. In any event, he came, he saw, he kicked.

Carter did it, too. In 1980 he said, "If Kennedy runs, I'll whip his ass." This anal fixation is clearly a bipartisan fetish.

I don't believe that Bush is a wimp in the textbook sense. I think a Hollywood phony who made Army training films and screwed starlets while brave men died is not only a wimp, but a hypocrite, considering his subsequently cavalier attitude about sending young men off to die for naught.

One of the youngest fighter pilots in the country's history isn't a wimp. Obviously, in later years, he can become a hack politician who thinks an off-color remark can convince the masses that he reeks of machismo.

He certainly lacks integrity. Does it take more courage to be an honest public servant than it does to engage in aerial combat? It would seem so. His conduct of late isn't that of an ass, but more like a real asshole.

JM

An Offer You Can Refute

Jesse Jackson, in an effort to explain black-on-black crime, attributed it to watching too many violent movies, and urged blacks not to go see the recently-released *Godfather III*.

The *Godfather* films are cinematic masterpieces that tell the powerful tale of an American tragedy. They comprise a thoughtful epic of Shakespearean scope. Since the movies are about the mob, there is violence, but it's not gratuitous violence. It's not there merely for the vicarious thrill, as it is in *Total Recall* and the *Die Hard* films; flicks I thoroughly enjoyed and own on home video.

These films have not, however, made me go out and bust heads or shoot people for their leather jacket or $150 sneakers. An antisocial idiot is an antisocial idiot regardless of his pigmentation or whether he watches Schwarzenegger or Mr. Rogers.

And why single out *Godfather III*, Rev? Maybe blacks shouldn't go to their local video stores and rent *Shaft* or *Superfly*, either.

NJN, whose musical tastes lean toward Karen Carpenter and Roger Whittaker, offers his opinion of a most antithetical genre.

My Rap On Rap

Some time ago, while walking my dog, a car pulled up alongside me. In it were two youths, blasting what they consider "music." They wanted me to meet their eyes. I chose not to and just ignored their noisy presence. They drove on, I'm certain, trying to find somebody — anybody — who might fall prey to their stereotypical form of intimidation.

A musical style, derivative perhaps of an old Chiquita Banana commercial, is hardly a threat to Bach and Beethoven's place in history, or a vocal threat to Belafonte, The Beatles, and Perry Como.

The animated banana in the commercial sang, "*I'm Chiquita Banana and I've come to say/Banana have to ripen in a certain way/But bananas like the climate of the tropical equator/so you should never put them in the refrigerator.*" The yellow fruit was rapping!

Although there are white Rap groups and fans, rap is essentially a black cultural phenomenon. Its "angry statement" music strikes a chord with angry kids who have, in some instances, reasons to be angry.

A strict diet of anger is counterproductive. Today's juveniles lionize these artists. Speak with a follower of rap, and another of "Heavy Metal." (Just the name hurts my ears!) They both argue with sincere conviction that their music contributes to social awareness. The Rap and Metal performers may sing about imminent environmental Armageddon, but that doesn't stop their faithful fans from throwing beer cans out of car windows. One has got to wonder what these throaty "philanthropists" are really contributing to the community-at-large.

And that's the rub. They could be accomplishing something truly amazing with their lyrics, since kids absorb them with a passion they don't ordinarily display for trigonometry. Instead, many of these so-called artists sing of sordid misogyny and profanity-laced violence to sell their albums and pack their concerts.

I told a youthful follower of Rap that Nat King Cole was, in many ways, a black pioneer. He was the first black to host a television show, and cowardly sponsors dropped out when bigoted pressures threatened their all-important profits. King Cole was a courageous trailblazer. Proving, of course, you can be a maverick and have a velvet singing voice. You can be unforgettable like Nat King Cole, or forgettable, like Snoop Doggy Dog.

NJN

And finally, I also took a musical icon to task.

Justify My $8.95 (plus tax)

When MTV announced that Madonna's latest video "Justify My Love," was too racy for their network, I was intrigued, but skeptical.

MTV airs some wild stuff, images to erect a teenage boy and enrage a feminist, so I figured Madonna must have gone over the top this time. When I heard she was releasing it as a video single right before Christmas, I realized that all the fuss was more artfully orchestrated hype from the Material Girl to make a few more million.

I bought it anyway.

The media warned me to expect explicit scenes of bisexuality, orgiastic sex, and sadomasochism. I was very disappointed.

There's one moment when Madonna is French-kissing another woman on a bed, but it's all too brief, and the other woman is mannish looking and sports a crew-cut. Now if Madonna was necking with a Kim Basinger-type . . . *ooh-la-la.*

As for the S&M, there are a few leather-clad folks milling about, and one where Madonna's real-life beau is strapped to a chair while one of the leather girls pulls his hair and sticks her tongue in his mouth.

Mild hijinks indeed!

Madonna's a naughty girl. I think she should be spanked for conning the throbbing masses into shelling out $8.95 plus tax for PG-13 rated mediocrity passing itself off as pop art. Filmed in black-and-white with a self-conscious, *artsy-fartsy* feel, it fails on all levels. It's pretentious, only remotely erotic, and it's a lousy song. And what does the black guy with the long fingernails doing the interpretive ballet symbolize?

The front page of a supermarket tabloid recently bore the headline: **I'M MADONNA'S KINKY SEX SLAVE. . .SHE TORTURES ME FOR KICKS!**

I can't wait for the video.

JM

1990

As students in a Catholic high school in The Bronx, New York, we were fed a brand of theology that we didn't quite buy. We were fed this line quite forcefully, with little chance to offer a rebuttal. Hence, during our mid-twenties, with the Progressive Pragmatist as a vehicle, we vented our respective spleens at the Roman Catholic Church, thereby exorcising the demons instilled by the priests and pedagogues, whose pious pontifications we had to silently endure. Neither of us is particularly religious these days, but neither are we "angry young men." We're both "spiritual" in our fashion, and concur with the line from Yeats, "The best lack all conviction, while the worst are full of passionate intensity."

Curb Your Dogma

"Your mind is cluttered with filth."
— my mother, upon reading *The Progressive Pragmatist.*

ABORTION IS A SIN, AND SO IS THE USE OF CONTRACEPTIVES.

The use of the latter prevents the former, but John "Condom" O'Connor and his less ubiquitous colleagues want it both ways. They want to lock your chastity belt and keep the key, returning it only if you agree to abide by their rules regarding romping.

AIDS IS A BIG PROBLEM, BUT SAFE SEX IS IMMORAL.

That's what the US Catholic Bishops proclaimed at their latest convention. These guys have presented progressive position papers in the past. They're against nuclear war (and got yelled at for saying so!). However, when it comes to matters sexual, medievalism rules. Auxiliary Bishop Austin Vaughan of Orange County, New York wanted to include a passage in their statement suggesting that AIDS is a form of divine punishment. Good sense prevailed, and the passage was not included, but the bottom line remains clear: You can only have sex when you're married, and only for procreational, not recreational, purposes. Fooling around just for fun, and in manners that don't promote the union of sperm and egg, are a no-no.

A priest/theologian on CNN's *Crossfire* said that it was better to die of AIDS than use a condom, because slipping on a rubber sheath is a mortal sin. I believe that such ideas are hatched in the minds of malevolent maniacs, and a God who would concur with such obscenity is no God of mine.

Another recent controversy, involved California State Assembly woman Lucy Killea, who was banned from receiving Holy Communion by her bishop, Leo T. Maher, because of her pro-choice stance. She represents a constituency that includes many non-Catholics, and to impose Church doctrine on non-believers is something they used to do, with excruciating success, during the Inquisition. People once feared that JFK would be taking orders from the Vatican. This wasn't the case, but current pressure applied by the Church onto Catholic politicians will revive old fears and prevent honest and able practicing Catholics from entering public service.

I don't see how the Holy Communion ban can be enforced. Will they hang wanted posters of Assemblywoman Killea in churches across the land? Anyone can walk up to any altar and receive the body and blood of Christ, no questions asked.

Actually, it's really bread and wine. Consuming human flesh is called cannibalism, and is, for the most part, frowned upon these days. Drinking human blood is usually limited to vampires. Send it to a lab for analysis, and it's still bread and wine. Swallow a host and it doesn't taste like meat. Drinking blood won't get you high (though a few shots of mine might give you a buzz), but drink some sacramental wine and you'll feel mellow.

What's the matter with you guys?!? Your fellow priests are being disemboweled in Central America. Man is poisoning the world God hath created. There are more important issues you can direct your energies toward solving. Forgo your morbid fascination with the many modes of genital stimulation.

You're a truly uptight crew. Your frustration is making you quite cranky. If you won't allow a significant other to bring you to climax, try the five finger exercise. It works for me.

God has more important things on Her mind than who's sleeping with whom!

A word to the wise: Ignore these guys! Do unto others as you'd have 'em do unto you, and enjoy yourselves. Life's too short to be bothered by a bunch of irascible old men in black.

JM

Confessions of a Lapsed Catholic

Walking the streets of the beautiful Bronx on Wednesday, February 28th, I observed a large number of passersby with smudges of dirt on their foreheads. And this meant only one thing to me, a baptized and bred Catholic: It was Ash Wednesday, the first day of the 40 day Lenten season that climaxes with Easter Sunday. Fifteen years ago, I'd have "given up" something for Lent, like bubble gum. Times change.

Nevertheless, being a sentimental guy, I became a touch wistful, remembering the days when I would get the charred remains of Palm Sunday's leaves thumbed onto my head in the Sign of the Cross. The priest, who went from person to person with what resembled a gold-plated ash-tray, would say something like, "You were dust; unto dust you shall return." I always wanted a big blotch, and hoped it would last the entire day. Religious symbolism can be fun at times, particularly to an impressionable youngster. A combination of ignorance and imagination creates an aura of transient spirituality.

The Lenten season usually meant a visit to the confessional for us grade-schoolers. The petrified pupils were led, one by one, into the equivalent of a photographer's darkroom. There we began, "Bless me Father, for I have sinned," proceeding to list our monumental misdeeds (fighting with brother, cheating at Monopoly, calling an old crab an "old crab"). Our penance: 10 "Our Fathers," 12 "Hail Marys," and an Act of Contrition. The numbers game. . .

Actually, I never knew a peer who looked forward to going to Sunday Mass, or who got a spiritual high from the 45 minute ceremony. After all, with the exception of the priest's sermon, Mass was a tiresome repeat. I was always more fond of television reruns, and still am. The terminal theological chatter was more than my prepubescent brain could tolerate.

Weekends were short, sandwiched between the misery of seemingly endless school weeks. Sunday service was an unwelcome nuisance.

Why do so many people get offended when others criticize or ridicule their religious faith? *New York Newsday*, a so-called liberal daily, rejected a cartoon by its regular illustrator that featured Cardinal O'Connor with staff in hand, but a coat-hanger at the end of it. The editor reasoned that it "went over the line." What line is this? Is Cardinal O'Connor God? He's just a guy, like you and me. No human being in a position of power and prominence should be exempt from criticism and commentary.

If I were a true believer in my baptized faith, I wouldn't condemn non-believers to an eternal roasting in the Abyss. The folks who get enraged at "heretics" great and small are obviously theologically insecure. If they were absolutely convinced in the power of prayer and eternal life, they wouldn't get too worked up over the infidel dogs who dare milk their sacred cows. They might pray for our souls, and that'd be nice. But they wouldn't stew in their sanctimonious juices.

It has been my Catholic experience that many church-goers merely attend Mass as an insurance policy. God just might be up there: checklist in hand.

If roasting like a pig at a Hawaiian luau is in the offing for me, the cast of characters who'll join me in this eternal cookout are a much more interesting crew than the frenetic faithful who'll sprout wings and catapult into the Heavens.

NJN

You Squat -- He'll Thrust

Those who can't do, teach.
And those who can't teach, teach gym.
Woody Allen

Good teachers teach. Great teachers inspire. And I like to think of myself as a great teacher.
-one of my high school gym teachers

You heard the hoopla and saw the stars on the recent "Earth Day" television specials in April. Rockers singing for the dwindling rain forests, comics lamenting the expanding ozone hole. Every celeb must prove he has a social conscience by adopting a cause, and it's not limited to left-leaning famous folk. Has-been Heston touts the NRA and shills for the *National Review*. A very pretty starlet, linked to pro-choice and environmentalist causes, has been romantically linked with Senator Alan Cranston (D-CA). (Hey, I'm not without kinks, but necrophilia is not among them.)

I have my own *cause celebre*: A truly relevant issue that dwarfs these other, comparatively minor concerns. I'm aggressively lobbying for national legislation which will insist that high school gym teachers be able to perform the exercises they inflict upon their students.

June marks the 10th anniversary of my release from high school. They were four lousy years from which I still suffer delayed shock syndrome, and the most godawful moments in that godawful nightmare were spent in gym class.

Twice a week I donned a white T-shirt and red shorts to be tormented by pig-ignorant sadists and frustrated athletes who released their repressed rage by humiliating the less-than-fit kids.

It was not "physical education." We were not permitted to go at our own pace and learn the correct ways to work out. You were worked till you dropped, and the first to fall were cruelly mocked by the dumb bastard with the whistle and their unsympathetic peers.

Guys become jerks in gym class. The locker room mentality seizes them and they swagger, cuss, bully the puny, and behave as if they've spent a few years on the *Lord of the Flies* island. Even I had to laugh at the nerdish youth who'd never seen a jockstrap and thought it was a shower cap, but I chuckled discreetly.

For two of the four years, my gym teacher was a stupid and nasty middle-aged galoot whose massive gut hung over his belt. He conducted class as if it were boot camp, strutting and bellowing like a half-baked drill instructor. If he had even attempted the regimen of push-ups, pull-ups, sit-ups, side-steps, four-count jumping jacks and the infamous "squat-thrusts" imposed on us, he'd have launched into a well-deserved coronary thrombosis, and not a soul would have offered mouth-to-mouth. The only thing this guy inspired was a deep distaste for gymnasia, and exercise in general.

Certain personalities shouldn't be allowed near kids. In freshman year, when showers were mandatory, we had to parade past this guy as he passed out the towels and stared expressionlessly through mirrored shades in the dimly lit locker room at all the naked 14-year-olds. In subsequent years most of us would rather stink than strip and shower after class. Even in my innocence, I sensed perversion afoot.

If gym teachers had to be fit enough to do the workout along with the class, such a man would be out of a job. And a fit, health-conscious teacher would most surely have accentuated the positive regarding exercise and nutrition, and not have turned the gymnasium into a chamber of horrors.

One final word about the phys. ed. instructor, an unholy throwback to the cave-dwelling Homo Erectus — *never turn your back on one when doing a squat-thrust.*

JM

Yahweh and Son

There have been many historic father-son relationships throughout the ages. The most important, and least explored, is the one between Yahweh and his boy, Jesus.

Yahweh was a mean old cuss in Biblical times, with a fiery temper. He believed in the pre-Horatio Alger work ethic. If you crossed him, God forbid, you paid dearly. You might be drowned, or if He was really agitated, turned into a pillar of salt. Creating the world in six days would make anybody cranky.

First things first: Was there a family resemblance between Yahweh and His youngster? It's hard to say. Yahweh was big on hiding behind clouds and abstract blurbs, speechifying while bushes were burning. A veritable Wizard of Oz. Son Jesus, on the contrary, was a people's deity, out on the streets for all to see. He had long hair, a scraggly beard, and wore a robe and sandals. A rather unkempt appearance. His dad, who preferred a low profile, had to be somewhat embarrassed.

Adding insult to injury, Yahweh's only child may have had an excessive thirst for the grape. Father, you should have known better. Never give a kid the power to turn water into wine! It's only asking for trouble. Yahweh may have liked imbibing "spirits" too, for He didn't always make sense. This could explain His self-description: *I Am Who Am*. What the hell does that mean?

New York Yankees owner George Steinbrenner seems more made in Yahweh's own image than son Jesus. The Lord Almighty demanded obsequious loyalty at all times. What He did to Abraham was hardly classy. Old Abe, in order to prove his allegiance to Yahweh, was told to sacrifice his own son as a sign of his unbending fealty. At the last moment, so the story goes, Yahweh stepped in, smugly satisfied. "Don't bother chopping off your boy's head," He said. In the meantime, Yahweh probably knocked a couple of hundred years off Abraham's life with the anguish attending the near-sacrifice. Abraham's premature death at 900 can undoubtedly be traced to Yahweh's little practical joke.

Since there were no Little Leagues 2,000 years ago, Yahweh's boy had to prove himself worthy by dying on the cross. Yahweh, in the image of Sam Breakstone, was one of the most demanding Dads alive.

Mercifully, Yahweh has stopped grumbling through the cirrostratus. In fact, deities all over the world seem to be holding back, whereas 20 centuries ago they were omnipresent nuisances.

Perhaps Yahweh has passed the torch to a new generation.

NJN

Let's Make It Official

John Cardinal O'Connor has warned Catholic politicians who are pro-choice regarding abortion that they are risking excommunication. A few hundred years ago, this kind of ecclesiastical blackmail carried much weight, and would have scared the hell out of any Medieval prince or pol. To a contemporary Secular Humorist, it remains an amusing, empty threat.

Johnny, I'm sure you'd have been happier in the Dark Ages, when clerics burned those who dared disagree. The days when infidels were converted at the point of a hot poker, poised to be inserted where the sun doesn't shine. When atrocities against God and Man, orgiastic license, the rape of nations and the theft of their riches and resources were committed in the name of Jesus Christ, the foremost critic of the organized religion of his day.

In "The Grand Inquisitor," a chapter of Dostoyevsky's epic *The Brothers Karamasov*, the Inquisitor sends Christ-come-again off to die again, because his presence will once again rouse the rabble and jeopardize the Church's very comfortable status quo.

I firmly believe that if you guys could still get away with the conduct of your predecessors, you wouldn't hesitate to impale, roast and disembowel your more vociferous critics.

I haven't been to Mass in quite some time, barring the occasional wedding and funeral, so I've more or less excommunicated myself. But a formal decree from Your Eminence would be a real treat. A document chock full of papal bull that I'd have laminated and displayed proudly on the wall. The ensuing publicity would be mutually beneficial. We're both shameless media-hounds who thrive on publicity.

Come on, Eminence. Be a pal, a good sport. I dare you, Johnny.

John Condom O'Connor: Excommunicate me. Please!

JM

The Bible

Three things are certain in this life: death, taxes, and human beings quoting the Bible to justify mistreating other human beings.

I had the recent misfortune of witnessing a battle of Biblical blowhards. One clique consisted of Jehovah's Witnesses, super-dedicated proselytizers and nuisances, seeking to convert the hapless heathens among us. The other group consisted of the mainstream Judeo-Christian consensus—those who attend church or temple regularly, yet still want to watch executions from their living rooms.

The Jehovahs religiously rambled on, as they're wont to do, and in their heavenly diatribe mentioned the "homeless." Within earshot, Mrs. Average American could stand no more. "I don't want to hear another word about those people. Let them reach rock bottom. That's the only way to improve their condition. The Bible says, 'He who doesn't work, doesn't eat.'"

Does the Bible say that? It sounds as fishy as Jonah, but then again, the Bible says we can fry people. Ever heard of "an eye for an eye?" But, wait a minute! What about "turn the other cheek?"

Throughout history, the Bible has been used to promulgate mischief and afflict misery on an awful lot of people. Slavery was practiced by many a biblical bloke, so why not still hold blacks in bondage? Women were second class citizens way back when, and if it was good for God's gander to treat geese as such, it's got to be par for the course today. Right?

I doubt very much that God is a schizophrenic. If the Bible is "divinely inspired," then God's not playing with a full deck. There are more contradictions in the Bible than there is a void between Dan Quayle's ears.

Maybe it was the translating into stone that caused the problem. The Almighty might fare better today if He inspired a few fellows with word processors.

Ideally, religion is about helping the helpless and conferring compassion on our neighbors. There's prose aplenty in the Bible to comfort the afflicted, and the truly pious out there have already zeroed in on what God is all about.

DT 13:6-10 makes it quite clear that under "God's law," a man is bound to slay members of his own family who are guilty of heresy.

Uh-oh!

NJN

Quote The Raving
special Cardinal O'Connor edition
"There is so much sex around."

Thus spake John Cardinal O'Connor to a group of school kids between the ages of five and fourteen. Once again, the Cardinal reveals his all-consuming fixation with carnal knowledge. He was griping about the NYC public school system's proposal to distribute condoms in the classroom in an effort to prevent unwanted pregnancies and the spread of AIDS. It is an acknowledgment that "just say no" doesn't work, and that kids will do as they please despite lectures, warnings and public service announcements.

Johnny The Card has warned that NYC is in danger of becoming *"Condom City."* Perhaps like Gotham City's Caped Crusader, he'd like to stalk the inner city by night, peeling rubbers off erections wherever he finds them.

There are greater social evils the Church should address, other than bedroom antics, but the old boys are monomaniacal in their determination to interrupt your coitus.

It's another case of the Church's inability to prioritize. The friction generated by unwed genital coupling is thought more monstrous than the fission that splits the atom. Two unmarrieds undulating under a sheet are more menacing than the words and deeds of a redneck robed in white.

They just don't want you to do it — period. Or only when and in what manner they deem fit. They're celibate control freaks who invoke God's name to thwart a little romping and romancing.

I think I understand the psychological dilemma of O'Connor and company. There's a scene in the movie *Revenge of the Nerds*, wherein a formerly stud-hungry cheerleader, having just made love to a nerd, is astonished by his passion. The nerd explains that, unlike the sports-obsessed jocks she's accustomed to, a nerd is obsessed with sex, thereby providing a more exuberant roll in the hay.

Girls of the world: Perform a truly selfless act of Christian charity and seduce a Cardinal. They've got years of pent-up libido waiting to be released. You'll probably have the ride of your life, and you'll do us all a big favor. If they realize what they've been missing, maybe they'll finally shut up and live and let live.

JM

Then How the Reindeer Loved Him

It's about that time of year again, when the networks dust off their holiday classics and air them *ad nauseam* until Christmas.

The best loved Yuletide special is, without a doubt, *Rudolph the Red Nosed Reindeer.* It's also the most damaging to young minds, and most of you parents probably didn't know that.

The puppet-mation makes "Rudolph" a treat for the kids. Burl Ives as an avuncular snowman in Christmas Town, serves as narrator. His scene-stealing ability rivals that of Rod Serling, Robert Stack, and William Dozier, and his rendition of "Holly, Jolly Christmas" is top notch.

That's where the entertainment ends and the poisoning of our youth begins. Rudolph is born with an impediment — his nose glows a fiery red now and then, and makes a squeaking noise when it does.

Rudy's father, Donner, immediately covers his honker with mud and tells his boy that he's going to look like everybody else, whether he likes it or not. Rudy, understandably, doesn't like his nose job. It's uncomfortable, and makes him sound funny. When he's old enough to join in the "reindeer games," his dark secret is revealed to all in an accidental fit of horniness, and he is painfully humiliated.

The young reindeer's ogre of a coach tells all assembled that "from now on, we won't let Rudolph play in any reindeer games."

Ol' St. Nick appears and tells Donner, "You should be ashamed of yourself!" The implication: You're a failure as a father because your son didn't turn out macho perfect.

What should the bearded fellow have done? He should have gotten up on his soapbox and proclaimed that "We are all God's children," or something to that effect.

He didn't. This particular St. Nick proved himself to be a chump extraordinaire. To start, he's a megalomaniac. The man sings, *"Jingle, jingle, jingle! I am ol' Kris Kringle; I'm the king of jing-a-ling!"* He calls himself a king! What an arrogant man!

Not only is the hapless Rudolph a victim of Christmas Town discrimination, but so is a non-conformist elf. He wants to be a dentist, not make toys for a living. Hence, he's a pariah, shunted aside, and given an ultimatum. Make toys or else. Or else what? The Christmas Town gulag?

Christmas Town is really a brutal dictatorship presided over by a despot in a red suit. Conformity rules.

Also worth noting: Santa Claus is razor thin on the eve of Christmas Eve. His matronly wife (whom he calls "mother"), tells him, "Who ever heard of a skinny Santa Claus?" The King of Jing-a-Ling, ornery to the end, finally relents and ravenously pigs out. On top of all his other vices, this Santa is a pig! Gluttony is one of the Seven Deadly Sins. Wouldn't a skinny Santa be preferable to one susceptible to heart disease, hypertension, and other obesity-related ailments?

Of course, there's a happy ending. After Rudolph and his "misfit" friends come back from their desertion of home, the town of non-thinking automatons has supposedly learned its lesson. Or has it?

Rudolph wasn't to be part of the reindeer team who pull Santa's sled, until a terrible blizzard hits Christmas Town. Desperate, Santa asked, "Rudolph, with your nose so bright, won't you guide my sleigh tonight?"

And as the song goes, "Then how the reindeer loved

him.. ." Then indeed! Now that you've proven useful, we love you.

"And I heard him exclaim as he drove out of sight: Merry Christmas to all, and to all a good night!"

NJN

Not only did we take religious figures to task in 1990, we were also quick to jump on Tipper Gore's (and most recently Bob Dole's) crusade against suggestive song lyrics.

A Legendary Performer

I never thought I'd find myself in agreement with the lovely Tipper Gore regarding the ability of song lyrics to corrupt impressionable minds. After listening to a particularly obscene recording recently, I'm afraid I must alter my anti-censorship stance.

I'm not talking about the grating cacophony of Heavy Metal or the bellicose chanting that is Rap. I'm referring to an entertainer who is the true Menace 2 Society.

Perry Como.

Yes, that beloved septuagenarian song stylist who has delighted listeners for decades. You've doubtless seen his holiday specials: Perry's *Easter in Hackensack*, his *Ash Wednesday at Sea World.*

Yet there's another side to the golden-tongued maestro. *Perry Como: A Legendary Performer*, available on RCA, is shocking in its flagrant sexuality. Perry's dulcet tones lewdly linger over such lascivious lyrics as:

I have a yearning to caress you/One thought keeps burn-

ing in my soul/A hungry yearning to possess you/It's far beyond control.

Strong stuff! "Yearning to caress" may lead listeners toward necking and heavy petting, which might result in "going all the way." "Yearning to possess you" clearly implies domination of the female, rather unfashionable in these liberated times. "Beyond control" suggests that Perry's lust may be uncontainable.

From another tune:

You were born to be kissed/I can't resist.

It seems we are privy to the internal ravings of a would-be rapist. A horny lad, upon hearing that girls are "born to be kissed," may act out his fantasies in an antisocial manner.

From the same song:

I'm just a slave; only a slave/To you: temptation/I'm your slave!

A clear reference to sadomasochism!

Another tune opens with the naughty command:

Beautiful girls/walk a little slower when you walk by me.

Why? Obviously so Perry can ogle their buttocks!

Finally, consider this little ditty:

Hot diggity, dog ziggity/Boom! What you do to me
It's so new to me/What you do to me/Hot diggity, dog ziggity/Boom! What you do to me/When you're holding me tight.

Unbelievable. A pop song about a man experiencing his first erection! Parents, if you pass the bathroom door and hear your son ejaculating, "Hot diggity, dog ziggity — BOOM!" from within, it's time for that birds-and-bees chat.

Perry Como leaves a legacy of songs implicitly advocating deviant sexual practices, rape, and masturbation.

Kids: Stay away from your grandparents' old LP's.

JM

And NJN began the gradual process of disillusion leading to downright disrespect for a fallen idol.

Et Tu, Mario?

The Republican Party fears Mario Cuomo. If they didn't, they wouldn't be dispatching stooges like Drug Czar William Bennett to snipe at the baggy-eyed Governor of New York.

Republican media consultants seem armed and ready for a 1992 Bush-Cuomo contest. They see it as a chance for the ultimate vindication of the conservative cause. The liberal media, they maintain, attributes the overwhelming defeats of Mondale and Dukakis to their ineptitude as campaigners and blasé-faire personalities, not their left-wing philosophies. Cuomo is the antithesis of that undynamic duo in temperament, and a landslide loss would mean the death of Liberalism once and for all. Strike three!

Cuomo, however, is not quite what he seems. He's a liberal jewel in an oratorical sense, but his lofty words don't match the dearth of his deeds. He plays the games all politicians play, and that's about the worst that could happen to a man of humble beginnings who has flirted with greatness.

In 1977 Mario ran for mayor of New York City. Touring the town in his Cuo-mobile, he dropped by my neighborhood, Kingsbridge, in the Bronx. He was then a veritable nobody from Queens. When he delivered his little speech, his ethnic charisma was reassuringly sincere, causing my teenage psyche to tingle with admiration.

Here stood an Italian-American speaking the language of compassion, but in a hard-nosed way. I had experienced familial populist conservatism all my life, and had never encountered an Italian man, with trade-marked rolled-up sleeves, who was a so-called liberal.

An angry fellow in the small crowd started heckling Cuomo at one point during the speech. He wanted Mario to explain his position on the death penalty. The future Governor paused, invited the heckler onto the Cuomobile platform, intimidating the man and effectively shutting him up. When he was finished speaking, I walked away from the event, leaving the candidate and his detractor in an even-tempered discussion out of earshot of the departing throng. Mario Cuomo was an impressive man, someone out of the ordinary. Quite unlike the horde of professional politicians who were seeking the mayoralty that year. *He has since joined the ranks of the professional politician.* In 1982 Cuomo slayed the philistine Ed Koch in the Democratic primary for Governor. His bid was labeled Quixotic when he announced his challenge of the rising star Koch. He beat Koch handily, running as a bare-faced liberal. He then defeated multi-millionaire Lew Lehrman in the general election. A man who spent $13 million (most of it his own), in an effort to rule in Albany.

Now Cuomo is the powerful incumbent with all the money. The New York State Republican Party is a sorry joke, evidenced by the absurd candidate that they finally dug up to challenge the Governor, Pierre Rinfret. Reportedly, 18 others declined to run before the powers-that-be settled for this little-known economist, not even registered in the Grand Old Party.

When Cuomo ran against another sacrificial lamb, the hapless Andy O'Rourke, he refused to debate him, unless certain ridiculous conditions were met.

Since the verbal triumph of Cuomo's speech at the Democratic National Convention in 1984, the man has proven to be no savior to the dedicated left-wingers who swooned around his altar of social idealism.

Cuomo's verbiage is titillating, to be sure. No one on the Democratic stage comes close to his oratorical finesse. And I'm going to vote for him in November. I may even be voting for him for President. But I'll be doing it with very little enthusiasm, and this I write with sadness as Ol' Baggy Eyes' former biggest fan.

NJN

"Causing my teenage psyche to tingle?!?" Hmmm. . .

And, finally, we pride ourselves as being one of the first publications to take on the ominous specter of Political Correctness. This caused some critics to accuse us of a shift to right, but we've refused to be defined by such labels. The McCarthy-ish tone of PC is nothing short of a New Fascism, and we are opposed to the Legislation of Ideas, whether it comes from the so-called Left or Right.

Enslaved by the Neo-Sensitive

Kid Cliché, upon sipping a warm, flat draft beer at Shea Stadium, exclaimed, "Nothin' like a cold one!" After igniting one of the malodorous nickel stinkweeds he bummed off me, he pronounced, "Nothing like a good cigar!" When things are going badly for the Kid, he shrugs his shoulders and opines, "Gotta have a sense of humor in this world."

On this score, Kid Cliché is quite correct.

When I was a lad in journalism school, some professors hailed me as "the young Jimmy Breslin." I was flattered to a degree, but humbly countered, "Breslin's a fat

Irish-American from Queens who drinks too much, and I'm a fat Irish-American from the Bronx who drinks too much, and there ends any similarity." Although he's not without wit, and I agree with him most of the time, when I see him on the tube he seems to have a sense of humor about all things save himself. Still, Breslin is to be credited for not bowing to the demands of the Neo-Sensitive.

Breslin writes a column for *New York Newsday*. In the May 3rd issue, he wrote a very obviously tongue-in-cheek tirade against working women. His wife is a NYC Council person, and he griped about how she's never home to perform her wifely duties. While not vintage Breslin, it provided a few chuckles.

A 25-year-old colleague at *Newsday*, Ji-Yeon Yuh, was not amused and fired off an internal memo accusing him of "spewing sexism." The gal is clearly a humorless stiff, or perhaps had a hidden agenda. Probably both, and her scheme paid off. Crybaby Breslin ran through the newsroom trashing her with foul-mouthed racist and sexist epithets. Called on the carpet for his unprofessional conduct, he was forced to issue an apology of dubious sincerity. That should have been the end of the incident, but it wasn't.

Ji-Yeon Yuh made the local TV rounds the next day demanding his hide. Asian-American groups demanded nothing short of the Chinese Water Torture. Yuh's remarks on radio and television indicated that she has a major chip on her shoulder, and was thoroughly enjoying her Warholian 15 minutes in the spotlight. During one radio interview, she told the tale of another *Newsday* editor, who was fired for saying much less than Breslin, and saying it to a friend in a bar! Off-duty and relaxing with a few cocktails, the drink often does the talking. Some scumball with an agenda overhears something and turns him in. And Ji-Yeon Yuh thought that was absolutely wonderful. This chick wants the Thought Police monitoring your every emotion.

Dear Ji-Yeon: *Shut Yuh Mouth!* You're 25 and have a damn good job. I'm 28 and would love to be a mild-mannered reporter for a major metropolitan newspaper. How'd you get the job, Affirmative Action? If you want to make a name for yourself, do it the way Breslin did, with talent and hard work. Enjoy it while it lasts, baby. You're a flash in the pan. It won't be long before you're working the salad bar in a Korean deli, and I'll be outside boycotting the joint.

To the Editors of *New York Newsday*: As founder and President of the Drunken Prose Poets Society, I demand the immediate dismissal of Ji-Yeon Yuh for her harassment of our poster boy, Jimmy Breslin.

And please find enclosed a copy of my resume for your consideration.

Editor's Note:

As publisher of The Progressive Pragmatist, I would like to express my deepest apologies for the previous rant, and assure you the Mr. Mannion has been suspended for two weeks without pay, effective immediately. His intolerance and insensitivity do not reflect the editorial policy and practices of The Progressive Pragmatist. I commend New York Newsday for putting the bloated blowhard Breslin in his place, and wish Ms. Yuh all the best in her future endeavors, and will be following her career with interest.

Nicholas J. Nigro

Publisher

A lot of our readers thought that NJN's wimpy reproof was a genuine article, not the ironical afterthought it actually was.

1989

NJN and I occasionally engaged in point-counter-point debates about issues of great importance to civilization as we know it. The following is one such clash of Titans.

A Joker For All Seasons

This summer's movie blockbuster *Batman*, starring Jack Nicholson and Michael Keaton, filled the coffers of Warner Brothers and many batty entrepreneurs peddling Batman paraphernalia to the fad-oriented, silly public.

The movie, however, should have more appropriately been called *The Joker*, for Jack Nicholson's *Clown Prince of Crime* stole the show. A good actor in an interesting interpretation.

When future generations think of The Joker, will they recall Nicholson's pasty white-faced character, or the father of the role, veteran character actor Cesar Romero?

Romero is The Joker for all seasons. Playing the role in the immensely popular 1960's series, Romero was the trailblazer that Academy Award winner Nicholson cannot surpass. The TV show's campy style offended comic book purists who believe that *Batman* should be treated with solemn reverence.

Though foolish people would disagree, Cesar Romero is the only Joker there will ever be. His role as "mischief maker. . . full of mad maneuvers," is on par with

Olivier's Hamlet.

It's time to give the man his due.

NJN

And I responded accordingly. . .

No Rabid Romero-phile, I

The *Batman* TV show is not the infantile silliness the comic book purists would have you believe; it contains sly satire and flashes of brilliant deadpan absurdism. It has the *BAM-SOCKO* hijinks for the kiddies and parody for the grown-ups.

And Cesar Romero, a former Latin lover of the '30's and '40's is a delight as the flamboyant, prancing dandy, The Joker. As this formerly straight-faced leading man approached his 60's in the '60's, he found the freedom to cut loose and expand his range as an actor.

When Mr. Romero attended a screening of the *Batman* movie, he lamented the film's violence, adding, "It's not the *Batman* concept at all. What we did was fun. It was a spoof. It was a comic strip."

Mr. Romero has missed the point entirely. The *Batman* comic book existed for 27 years before the TV show, and continues to enjoy great success. And it's not a spoof. The movie evokes the mood of the comics and Jack Nicholson's Joker is a very different interpretation than Romero's.

The movie isn't a comedy, though Nicholson is hilarious. There's menace in his madness — this Joker kills people. The TV Joker tries, but is hopelessly inept. He is more clown than criminal. Jack's Joker is a twisted maniac, disfigured by Batman and bent on revenge. And he's hysterically funny as he sings, dances and shamelessly hams it up. A lesser actor would have looked foolish, but Nicholson is the greatest living American actor and pulls it off flawlessly.

I like the old show, and Cesar's campy cavorting, but I give the movie, and Nicholson, the edge. It's a powerful, surreal, darkly compelling minor classic. Let the fanatics in either camp take potshots at each other; there is room for both.

Profound philosophizing, I'm sure you'll agree. We got a couple of nasty letters saying we had degenerated from our formerly politically conscious selves, but politics is a dry, maddening affair at times, and NJN and I were growing in the conviction that "fluff" is the true "good stuff" of life.
We did debate another issue, slightly less important than who was the better Joker: flag burning.

Mind If I Light Up?

People who burn flags are, invariably, skunks and low-lives. Our Constitution must sometimes protect the vile among us, to preserve the rights of the virtuous.

What are Americans afraid of, anyway? The American flag is desecrated every day in the dailies. Used car dealers picture Old Glory in their ads that push lemons on the public. Retail capitalists sell flags for profit. The federal government doesn't distribute them gratis with IRS refund checks.

So, how can someone stop another from desecrating his/her property, if he/she chooses? Granted, the flag is a powerful national symbol, and anyone torching it in public risks starting a full-scale riot. The Cross is a powerful religious symbol, and it is desecrated by hate groups on a regular basis. This is the price one pays for living in a more-or-less free society.

Predictably, the President wasted no time in jumping into the constitutional amendment clamor. "Flag burning is wrong," Bush said as he began a news conference.

No kidding, George, but have you ever considered that there are people who disagree with you, and if they want to reduce a flag to ashes as an act of political protest, the Constitution says it's okay.

The Constitution is what America is about, not a piece of cloth. Should an anti-flag burning amendment pass, Mr. President, you'll have a lot of questions to answer.

Are those flags on toothpicks that we decorate cakes with to be protected? What about a cake itself, with garish red, white and blue icing? Can we eat it?

NJN

Put That Match Out, You Fool!

Yes, the flag is symbolic, and the malcontents and misfits who burn it are lucky it's the American flag they're burning. Burning the flags of less tolerant nations will get you locked up in dank dungeons with tormentors who'll be giggling as they affix electrodes to your testicles.

Georgie B. gathered the media around him when he visited a flag factory, as smugly self-righteous a photo-op as they come, particularly when the objective was to impugn the other guy, portraying him as a card-carrying ACLU Red who is implicitly responsible for the rape of a white woman by a furloughed black hoodlum. This kind of sleaze is symbolic flag desecration.

Nationalize the flag factories, eliminate the trivialization of Old Glory through trashy merchandising, and distribute "official" flags free of charge to anyone who wants one, with the understanding that its intentional public destruction is a criminal offense.

Flag burning rubs every decent American the wrong way on a visceral level, including those who defend a person's right to do so. What the flag symbolizes is more important than the flag itself.

JM

Just when you thought you'd seen the last of Cardinal O'Connor trashing, we're back with two more pieces from 1989. NJN's article bears the witty title. . .

Cardinal Jerk

New York Archdiocese autocrat, John Cardinal O'Connor was up to his old tricks in the New York City mayoral race this fall.

The two candidates, Democrat David Dinkins, and Republican Rudolph Giuliani, marched in the Pulaski Day Parade one Sunday morning, that passed St. Patrick's Cathedral.

O'Connor greeted Dinkins warmly, telling him, "We've got to sit down. It's time for breakfast." Giuliani was given the ecclesiastical cold shoulder for all the world to see. "Cardinal Chills Rudy," the *Daily News* headline read the next day.

The Cardinal is a certified jerk. What's worse, he's a smug jerk. He is obsessed with abortion. Fine. Religious leaders have a job to do and an agenda to promulgate.

But what's this grandstand politicking about? Why, Cardinal, do you continue to sabotage Catholic politicians? Geraldine Ferraro was your first target. She was too much for you and yours to accept. Not only was she pro-choice on abortion, she was a *she*. And you ex-Navy chaplains obviously have a better rapport with seamen than members of the opposite sex.

Now Rudy Giuliani falls victim to the pious hack with the funny hat and expensive jewelry. O'Connor the "pro-lifer" endorsed David Dinkins, a "pro-choice" Protestant, but he denies it.

The Cardinal, speaking to the media in his usual hushed, reverent tone, said he doesn't like political opportunism. That is, Catholic pols who tailor their abortion stances to get votes. He said he wasn't referring to anyone in particular, but it was obvious that he was referring to Giuliani. Five Our Fathers and five Hail Marys for that fib, O'C.

Why the deception, Cardinal? Don your clown hat and full regalia, and maybe David Dinkins will let you be the court jester at his coronation.

NJN

Strong stuff, NJN! And you've called me the O'Connor-basher of the team. Why, I positively lob softballs by comparison, as you'll see in. . .

The Cardinal Sins

John Cardinal O'Connor put in his two cent's worth recently concerning "obscenity" on television. A reporter covering the Academy Awards quoted funnyman Robin Williams, who said that his pregnant girlfriend would be starring in the upcoming flick, "Fetal Attraction." Not vintage Mork, but the reporter and two anchors hooted at the wisecrack.

It seems that Johnny The Card was watching *Live at Five* that afternoon and steam shot out of his ears. He later devoted an entire sermon to the incident, calling television a "wasteland of filth," and chastised the news people for chuckling, suggesting that they wield influence as role models, and that unwed motherhood simply isn't funny.

Chill out, Eminence! Reserve your wrath for more weighty matters. Television as wasteland is a legitimate criticism, but you're wrong to cite the plastic personalities who populate the airwaves as role models. Those who would see them as such are dummies beyond salvation, and a comic's silly remark is not symbolic of the moral decay of Western Civilization.

I'm sure you received a standing ovation from abortion clinic bombers, but to the sane brain you come across as a cranky old fart raving about innocuous trivialities.

Laughter is the best medicine: Cardinal, heal thyself.

JM

Goodbye, Farewell, and Amen

Ronald Reagan's farewell address to the American people was hardly in the tradition of George Washington.

On September 17th, 1796, the *Daily American Advertiser* of Philadelphia, published the President's parting shot. No television; Americans had to read the address — penned with the help of future President James Madison and Alexander Hamilton.

In Washington's adieu, the outgoing President warned of establishing "permanent foreign alliances." He cautioned Americans on inter-party squabbling that might harm the national interest. He counseled the new country against relying on an "over-powerful military establishment," similar to Eisenhower's "military-industrial complex" warning almost two centuries later.

Reagan's recent good-bye was noteworthy for its lack of electricity. The B-actor turned grade-A in the White House. We thought he would turn in the performance of his career as he said bye-bye. We thought he'd have legions from sea to shining sea in tears as he rode into the proverbial sunset. "Everything's wonderful now, thanks to me," was the gist if it. He even referred several times to the "Reagan Revolution."

When the President attempted to sum up his performance, he simply said, "Not bad. Not bad at all." And off he went.

Thanks for nothing, Ronny.

NJN

NJN sent an issue of The Progressive Pragmatist to a friend of his family, who also happened to be a Catholic priest whom I knew from my an altar boy days. I suppose he was hoping to drum up some business, and gain another subscriber. Unfortunately, the issue he sent the Rev included this article of mine. He hasn't heard from "Father B." since.

Few Are Called, Less Are Chosen

When I was a kid in Catholic school, we were told that those who chose the religious life received a "calling" from the Almighty. Evidently, "She" is having trouble with the line, because few are called and less are chosen these days. When the Church relies on Madison Avenue rather than the Holy Spirit to recruit potential celibates, you know it's having problems.

Fortunately for Holy Mother Church, this lapsed lad has the solution — give His Holiness and the College of Cardinals some sacramental wine, and while they're nice and mellow, get them to abandon their archaic, asinine attitudes.

Why no sex? Other religions allow their reverends and rabbis to wed, and their flock doesn't suffer as a result. It's a stupid policy that should be summarily stricken from the record. Let them do the horizontal dance, and watch the seminaries fill. Even "deacons," lay quasi-clerics who help out because of the priestly shortage, have their bedroom antics restricted. If you're a bachelor who becomes a deacon, you can never marry, and if you're a married deacon who becomes a widower, you can never remarry. Why, why, why this unnatural fixation on what couples do between the sheets?!?

Why no women? There's nothing like a dame.

Nothing in the world, and if a modern woman wants to contribute more, what's the big stink? Women had an extremely active role in the early days of the Church, when its members were hunted down and fed to felines. But when it became **the** religion, and started doing the same to those who disagreed with them, women resumed their second class citizenry. There are plenty of faithful and capable women out there. Personally, I'd rather see Jane Cardinal O'Connor any day.

Dear Mr. Pope: Looks like it's time for Vatican III. The significant changes of Vatican II were not divinely inspired, as many claim. They were made because people were bolting from the pews in droves, and Holy Mother Church was getting a royal pain in the collection plate.

As a multi-billion dollar empire, the Church has got to adapt to the New Age to survive. Tell 'em it's okay to fool around. Turn the other cheek when a guy slips on a rubber. Give the gals a more active role in all that Papal Bull. You'll get more fans, your staff will grow, and you'll increase your bottom line.

JM

NJN was always bi-partisan in his criticism of political phonies. In these next two articles, he gives it to the then-President and the omnipresent senior Senator from Massachusetts.

Where Is George?

Verbosity leads to unclear, inarticulate things.
— Dan Quayle

Last year, a Presidential candidate with a penchant for putting his foot in his mouth, was being roundly denounced as a non-entity by the opposition. "Where was George?" was the rallying cry of hopeful Democrats.

A year later, George Herbert Walker Bush is the 41st President of the United States, but you might not know it. You knew where Ronald Reagan stood from the get-go. He was palling around with the Bloomingdales and the Annenbergs. He appointed a Dragon Lady to head the Environmental Protection Agency and a creature from outer space to head the Department of the Interior. People who went to soup kitchens were called freeloaders, and ketchup was classified as a vegetable. The Attorney General under Reagan said a suspect of a crime was presumed guilty.

At least Reagan stood for something.

What George Bush plans to do for the next four years is anybody's guess. Like a parent with a troubled child, Bush has got Danny Quayle to fret over. *Newsweek*, for example, publishes a chronology on interesting and offbeat statements made by people in the news. Almost weekly, the Vice President utters something silly, some might even say dumb. On his Latin American tour, Quayle wistfully regretted not keeping up with his Latin studies in school. It's a knee-slapper, all right, until the reality sets in that this guy is a "heartbeat away."

Bush is the product of a bogus campaign where we were given a black-and-white choice: Dukakis, the unpatriotic leftist versus the "all-American" Bush.

Demagogues are out there, preying on the populace's penchant for wanting easy answers to complex questions.

NJN

Senator Brain Dead

When Senator Ted Kennedy came to New York this past September to endorse mayoral candidate David Dinkins over Ed Koch, he drew some cheers, as a Kennedy inevitably will.

It was obvious on this day, that Kennedy was past his prime as a political force. More accurately, he was an embarrassment, particularly to "practical liberals" who'd rather not be lumped together with the bloated Senator from Massachusetts.

"I know what Robert Kennedy would say if he were here now," the clairvoyant Kennedy said at the news conference endorsing Dinkins. "Some see things in New York as they are and say 'why?' David Dinkins sees this city as it can be and says, 'why not?'"

Teddy's grave-robbing again. Who's been programming this stumblebum these days? Transposing Bobby Kennedy's moving words of two decades ago was silly and cheap, yet typical of the baby brother of the Kennedy clan.

"Ed Koch is the great divider", the Senator intoned, "David Dinkins is the great healer." Such robotically-delivered clichés have become the staple fare of Kennedy.

At Robert Bork's Supreme Court confirmation hearings, Senator Kennedy was at his brain-dead worst. Rather than confronting the nominee with pointed questions and follow-ups, and thus exposing Bork as the Neanderthal he is, Teddy just raved on about how "blacks would be seated in the back of the bus," and women "would be confined to the kitchen."

Happy 20th anniversary, Ted! Yes, it has been 20 years since you made skid marks on the Dyke bridge traveling at "eight miles per hour." There are indeed two systems of justice — one for the rich and powerful and one for the rest of us.

Ted Kennedy as "the champion of the oppressed" is absurd. How many barroom brawls and waitress-fornicating encounters will it take to destroy his credibility? From JFK to TK, the Kennedy boys have treated women rather shabbily. With a cornucopia of girlfriends on the side and baby-making wives at home, they don't exactly embody the feminist ideal.

Burton Hersh, stooge-biographer and author of *The Education of Edward Kennedy*, wrote bizarrely of the Chappaquiddick tragedy, where six single women in their twenties partied at a summer cottage with five married men and one aged, unmarried chauffeur. Hersh condescendingly concluded that the Senator would not have had any sexual interest in those "plain girls" who attended the cookout. Surely, if he had planned an orgy that evening, prettier pictures would have been in order. How Kennedy-esque and demeaning to women!

Is Congressman Joseph Kennedy III the heir apparent to his uncle's Senate seat? Has he the qualifications: shallowness, a roving eye, shrillness, reckless driving? Hmmm. . .

NJN

Once again, compelled to put politics on paper, I elected to approach it from a different angle than my colleague.

Help Wanted: Male

Those horny Congressguys are at it again: Republican Buzz Lukens gets nailed on a statutory rape rap, and Democrat Barney Frank gets caught with his pants down. If a fella has an itch that needs to be scratched, who are we to say nay? However, if the lady in question is 16, even 16-going-on-35, that is a no-no, and a pol's a schmoe to risk such indecent exposure. Buzz got what he deserved, but what of Barney?

The uncloseted New Englander admitted that he solicited the services of a male prostitute. So, he has to pay for it. He's no Kevin Costner. I just hope for Barney's sake that he practices safe sex. The boy-strumpet is over 18, a consenting adult, but most johns don't invite hookers to move in with them, pay them 20K a year, and remain blissfully ignorant of the fact that they're continuing to turn tricks under their roof.

Dumb move, Barney, and although intelligence has never been a prerequisite for holding elected office, such boneheadedness might merit a pink slip in the next election. It's not about sex; it's about smarts, and Frankly Barney seems lacking on that score.

These sleazy episodes, have, however, inspired me. Since this progressive musing is strictly *pro bono* work, and I'm currently "between positions," please excuse a little advertising:

Attention Congressgirls under 45!

Preferably Democrats, but I'm bi-partisan in bed. Are you looking for a politically correct, Sean Connery look-alike (circa

"Goldfinger")? Look no further! Huggable, eclectic, tough/tender pundit. No Donahue/Alda sissy, but no knuckle-dragger, either. Am willing to relocate to Beltway, am seeking politically rising star to be employer/companion, etc. Am into hand-holding, classical music, three-plus martini lunches. Typing 35 wpm, great interpersonal skills, ability to interface with everyone from pages to Prez. Available for after-hours, candlelight confabs, lobbyist-paid Caribbean junkets. Can out-shred Fawn Hall. You name it ma'am : This Guy Friday aims to please. The testosterone is flowing, babe — let's explore our fantasies. Resume and references available upon request. No Bella Abzug-types need respond.

JM

NJN bids adieu to a New York Mayor, whose entertainment value exceeded his administrative acumen.

Goodbye, Mr. Ed

When all the votes were counted on September 12th, NYC voters had at long last served an eviction notice on their beleaguered, loudmouthed Mayor Ed Koch. He was defeated in the primaries by David Dinkins, who beat Rudolph Giuliani to become the city's first black mayor.

Koch's concession speech was without rancor and uncharacteristically humble. It was a speech many thought he'd never have to give. He had often spoken about having the job for life. Koch's brother Harold once remarked that he didn't know what his sibling would do if he wasn't mayor. He said, in so many words, that brother Ed would shrivel up and die, were he ever ousted from office.

Koch was a sorry spectacle in conceding defeat. Surrounding him on-stage were a host of politicians and political appointees. No wife, no children, and probably few real friends. Bachelor Koch was married to the mayoralty, and had just lost his spouse of 12 years.

It was fitting that he was surrounded by pols and more pols. The man ate, drank and slept politics — it was his Life. And the city crumbled around him while those pol-pals ransacked its coffers.

Farewell, Eddie. Go get a talk radio show, and we'll name a park after you.

NJN

NJN wasn't through with making fun of poor old former President Reagan. He followed Reagan's post-Presidential shenanigans with equal malice. File this one away under "Cheap Shot."

A Dutch Treat!

Not long after his horse threw him for a loop, former President Reagan was back in the broadcast booth after half a century's absence.

At the behest of his California neighbor, the vainglorious Vin Scully, Ronald Reagan agreed to call an inning of baseball's Mid-Season Classic. It was hyped as a trip down *Memory Lane.*

The former President can kiss Goodbye any future broadcasting career. His one inning of flustered near-muteness beside the obsequious Scully was painful to observe. The doddering Reagan was served up softball after softball by Scully. The retired Chief Executive swung and missed every one.

The NBC hierarchy must have assumed that getting Reagan was a real coup. An open request to network bigwigs: Let Ronny be! Let him enjoy his golden years on the ranch without thrusting him upon those of us trying to escape reality for a few hours of baseball.

If Reagan and Scully want to remain a television duo, their best bet is becoming spokesmen for a hair-dye product.

NJN

Oh, you nasty man!

Here's my commentary on royalty, and a reflection on my roots.

Off With Their Heads!

As an anti-monarchist and *Secular Humorist* of Irish extraction, it irks me terribly when I see American statesmen bowing and scraping before England's royal family, the highest-paid welfare recipients in the world.

Protocol be damned! We threw off the yoke of mad King George two centuries ago — they deserve no deference. I hold in high regard the Cockney laborer who struggles to provide for his family while being victimized by England's caste system, not some upper-crust twit who has never worked a day in his life.

English kings, princes, and politicians have shat upon the little island Ireland for 1,000 years, and have done so by claiming Divine Right of Kings — God himself made them boss while the serfs must wallow in the cow dung. Attempted Celtic genocide, the exploitation of India and the rape of Africa — this is the legacy of the Crown of England. The arrogant and antiquated notion of monarchy should not be honored by American politicians and diplomats.

Storm the Bastille, citizens!

JM

Asked to write about George Bush, this is the best I could come up with. Author's note: This is political satire. In Swiftian fashion, I don't really mean everything I say in this next piece.

Ask a Wounded Squirrel

Since this paper's conception, I have written pieces that some might consider critical of Ronald Reagan. Indeed, I have found little to redeem the old geezer and his unsavory crew of fascists, hypocrites, villains and fools. But a little gem in the notorious *New York Post* recently has caused me to ever-so slightly re-evaluate The Gipper and question, the "kinder, gentler" nature of the aged preppie who has Bush-whacked us all.

According to the *Post's* gossipy "Page Six," Grandpa Ron regarded the squirrels on the White House grounds as pets, often carrying a bag of peanuts to feed them. Georgie B., on the other hand, sees them as fair game for his dog, and as Veep he credited the canine with "five live kills." One cannot fault the mutt — it's acting out of instinct — but Georgie's delight in the slaughter reveals a mean streak.

I, like Ron, enjoy the relaxing avocation of squirrel-feeding. There's nothing more quietly satisfying than strolling through the park with Walkman, six-pack, and big bag of peanuts for the cute little critters. No rabid rodent-phile I, but the tree-dwelling furballs are charming and inoffensive beasts.

Grandpa Ron knew this. They're God's creatures. The hell with the homeless bums, loonies, junkies and drunks — they either prefer or deserve their lot. But Grandpa Ron would never deny a nut to a squirrel, for he's a lovable lug with a big heart.

So, when Bush and Gorby sit down for tea on the White House lawn, and the President's pedigreed pooch approaches with a squirrel in its jaws, its broken bones and steaming entrails soiling the linen, let Georgie convince Gorby that it is indeed a kinder, gentler, world he strives for.

JM

NJN observes the Shakespearean credo, "Brevity is the soul of wit," in this collection of. . .

Miscellaneous Musings

· When Lazarus rose from the dead, he probably looked like liberal pundit and CNN *Crossfire* star Tom Braden.

· Former National Security Adviser Zbigniew Brzezinski, on why he never ran for office: "I didn't want to beg for money from obnoxious rich people."

· Mayor Marion Barry of Washington, DC, has taken decisive action in the war on drugs by establishing "illegal drug zones." Where, Mr. Mayor, are the "legal drug zones?"

· It's great to see President Bush giving lip service to the drug problem. Delivering a major speech on the subject in Amish Country helps a lot. We all know about the big cocaine problem there.

· Newt Gingrich: This little weasel, named after an

amphibian, is setting himself up for a fall. His partisan "ethics" crusade will likely backfire.

NJN's infamous precognizance strikes again! As of this writing, Gingrich is Speaker of The House and more powerful than ever. It's a good thing NJN turned his talents to writing about old TV shows. I get another chance to rant about my unhappy high school experience in the following bitter memory.

Stupid Asinine Test

Standardized tests are for standardized minds.

Some say they're racially biased, but I disagree. I'm a white guy and I did lousy on them. Maybe I didn't fully fill in the oval. Maybe I didn't use a No. 2 pencil. My performance on computerized exams was mediocre at best. On essay exams, when required to form coherent ideas and express them in literate sentences, I must humbly concede that I performed with distinction.

The SAT (Scholastic Aptitude Test) is the deciding factor in getting into a good college. It's divided into two sections: English and Math. The highest you can get is 800 in each, for a total of 1600. I got a fair-to-middling 600-English, 400-Math. One of my teachers flatly informed me that my life was shot to hell. A questionable college (perhaps I shouldn't even bother), menial job and miserable life were in store.

He was wrong.

When I was doing hard time at a Catholic high school in the Bronx, way back in the 1970's, they took the honor students and put them in an intensive preparatory program to help boost their SAT scores. Kids who would have scored high anyway were helped to score higher still.

They were taught ways to beat the system, techniques to employ and traps to avoid by going over old versions of SAT tests. It had nothing to do with the pursuit of knowledge; they learned tricks to beat the system.

I have often wondered why they didn't give kids with the lowest grades the opportunity to take this program — hence giving them a chance at a better education, career, and life. Were we dismissed as losers not worthy of the effort, an academic example of Christ's "the poor will always be with us" observation?

Being in the unhappy median, neither brainiac nor dullard, I just muddled through, counting the days till I got the hell out of high school. I bore the psychological terrorism with Promethean endurance, knowing one day that my time would come.

It has, and I've only just begun.

JM

We conclude 1989 with perhaps the strangest piece ever to appear in The Progressive Pragmatist. It is called "Designer Dependency," and the name "J. Mannion" appears below it. After six years, it's time to blow the lid off this shocking cover-up. I had promised to write a piece for NJN about celebrities in drug and alcohol rehabs, but I was too — how shall I say — "indisposed" to write it. NJN ghostwrote it, attempting to mimic my inimitable style, and slapped my name on it. And nobody knew the difference! This was the moment I "hit bottom" as an active alcoholic, and had my "moment of clarity."

Designer Dependency

What, you've never been chemically-dependent? What an insignificant non-entity you are!

In a perverted sense, this is the unintentional message the Hollywood jet-set, and moneyed world of sports is sending, via the increasingly moronic media.

A public persona who's flushed her diet pills down the toilet, or terminated his 90-proof liquid diet, is assured *cause-célèbre* status.

When Betty Ford courageously came out of her White House closet, admitting she was held hostage by adult beverages and pharmaceuticals, she helped many an average schmoe exorcise his/her mind-altering demon.

Today the Betty Ford clinics of the country are being exploited by some disreputable juicers and their pill-popping soul mates. These publicity-craving big shots, in effect, sell their drug rehabilitation stories for a feature spot on *Entertainment Tonight*.

I would gladly swap my prodigious thirst for a few (and a few more) cold ones, for a grog-free body, were life a multiple choice quiz. Regrettably, existence isn't so easily reduced to choices a, b, or c.

My real beef with "recovery mania" stems from its cancerous growth in tabloid journalism — be it of the boob tube variety or *People Magazine* frivolity. Appearances on Oprah, Phil, Pat, and Arsenio are par for the course for the formerly-crocked celebrity.

And guess what, the presently high-flying, formerly soused star of stage and screen, or formerly pickled pol, may someday return to the doldrums of despair. And round two won't be conducted in a *Rocky* story climate, for the fickle public does not pull for two-time boozers.

Freedom from premature embalming, non-

Parkinson's disease shakes, nausea, and diarrhea are liberating notions. But, wearing the proverbial brand that reads, "I'm recovering from a chemical dependency," is nauseating.

And, if I have to get nauseous, I'd prefer getting there the old-fashioned way.

"J. Mannion"

Who is "Pat" in the "Oprah, Phil, Pat, Arsenio" list? Don't ask me -- I glided through the 1980's in a blackout.

1988

NJN discusses a President and his heir apparent in the next two pieces, front page articles that I affectionately came to call the "long, boring articles." That's just my opinion, however. Read on. . .

The Old Man and The "C"

Ronald Reagan has been President for seven long years. He's largely irrelevant at the present time, and not because the calendar tells us he's 77-years-old. Ronald Reagan was an old man 30 years ago, in philosophy and attitude, when, for example, he likened JFK to Karl Marx. Philosopher-jock Yogi Berra once remarked, "It ain't over till it's over." As far as the so-called "Reagan Revolution," is concerned, however — it's over!

Remember Jimmy Carter; his Presidency seems eons ago. The man from Plains was in large part responsible for the rise of Reagan. Carter was perceived as incompetent. Reagan seemed a robust contrast. He coasted into office with a promise to balance the federal budget and wreak havoc on terrorist aggressors.

Jimmy Carter, a nuclear physicist and voracious reader, was a brilliant man. Yet he failed to master the leadership mode. Americans figured they'd go for a man who boasted that he was a lackluster student. Reagan told us forthrightly that, as an undergraduate at Eureka College, he was interested in sports, and little else, and that he was a consistent "C" student.

He reached the top riding a wave of born-again fervor, a new phenomenon in the voting booth. Those who longed for a return to "traditional values" were Reagan's loyal boosters, even though Ron was the first divorced President, and his family life can't be compared with the Waltons.

Missing in action at the White House these last seven years — the old-style news conference. Who can forget the shouting press minions vying for attention? We've had Reagan and the red carpet, instead. When The Gipper opts for a rare get-together with the press, he strides in like a septuagenarian weight-lifter. He tried a seating chart a couple of times, calling on members of the fourth estate as if they were fourth graders.

Remember the infamous triumvirate of Meese, Deaver, and Baker? Today, Meese, the nation's chief law enforcer, is the subject of two major criminal investigations. One inquest concerns Meese's role in the Wedtech case and whether he used his official position for personal profit. The other delves into Meese's role in the Ollie North scandal.

Deaver, stood trial for influence peddling and perjury. His defense: Alcoholism. How did Jerry Falwell feel about this? He was once quoted as saying, "They (liberals) call it alcoholism; we (conservatives) call it drunkenness."

The last of the Big Three, James Baker, is currently Treasury Secretary. And lo and behold, he has accomplished what few men could — he has made his raging bull of a predecessor, Donald Regan, look appealing.

Portents of things to come were evident in 1981, when Reagan nominated James Watt to be Secretary of the Interior. Watt informed a House Committee that, since Christ's Second Coming was imminent, he wasn't too worried about the decimation of our natural resources.

Howard Baker was Senate Majority leader when Reagan assumed power. He's now White House Chief of Staff. He called the Reagan economic program a "riverboat gamble" when it was enacted. He's now referred to by Senator Orrin Hatch of Utah as a "gutless wonder," for not allowing "Reagan to be Reagan."

Radio personality Paul Harvey coined the expression "Reaganomics." It is an apropos description for a haphazard program that has given us recurring $200 billion budget deficits, a mammoth military budget, cuts for the poor and students. To be fair, there has been sustained economic growth, lower inflation and interest rates. But lest we forget, 1982 saw the worst recession since the Great Depression. "Nancy gets a red dress, we get pink slips," the buttons read.

It has often been lamented by Reaganauts that the President received a mandate to implement his policies, only to be stymied left and right by a recalcitrant Democratic Congress. Why, they've bemoaned, have Democrats thwarted the President's ability to govern?

What kind of mandate exists when New Jersey votes 60%-39% to re-elect the President, while simultaneously giving its liberal Senator, Bill Bradley, 64%? What kind of mandate was decreed by the people of Massachusetts, who gave the President 51% in 1984, but also elected a soul mate to Ted Kennedy, John Kerry, with 55%? Two years later they re-elected their Democratic Governor, Michael Dukakis, with 69%. New York State gave Ronald Reagan 54% in his re-election bid, and two years later gave Mario Cuomo 65%.

One more year of lame-duckery and the Reagan years are history. The legacy of this out-of-touch Chief Executive points to the need for a US version of parliamentary democracy. The Reagan Administration, in a set-up similar to Great Britain's, would have fallen in the wake of the Iran-Contra fiasco, and a new election would have been called. This would eradicate the lame-duck factor, which often cripples second-term Presidents. Since this is not likely to happen, we'll have to be content with the 22nd Amendment, brought to us courtesy of the 1948 Republicans, limiting a President to two terms.

NJN

The Adventures of Silly George

"We're going to — the MX — we're going to have to do that. It's Christmas. It's Christmas. Wouldn't it be nice to be so perfect?"
— George Bush, calm and collected, in the first Presidential debate, 9/25/88

Who made the Pledge of Allegiance a campaign issue and then bungled in trying to recite it? Who called himself an environmentalist after chairing a Presidential task force on regulatory relief that proposed easing or eliminating 35 regulations on auto emissions and safety? Who advertised his decision-making ability after picking an unfit *Ken Doll* as his running mate? If you answered George Herbert Walker Bush, the man with as many names as home towns, this Bud's for you.

Silly George's campaign of liberal-bashing and flag-waving phoniness has demonstrated why politics is sometimes called the "world's oldest profession." Silly George has prostituted himself to win an election.

Silly George recites the Pledge of Allegiance to a gallery of mannequins at the Republican National Convention. They cheer. Silly George speaks quasi-coherently of the American Civil Liberties Union in the first Presidential debate: "I simply don't want to see the ratings of movies — I don't want my grandchild to go into an Xrated movie. I like those ratings systems. I don't think they're right to try to see kiddie pornographic laws repealed. I don't want to see 'under God' come out from our currency."

Silly George cruises Boston harbor in an effort to embarrass his opponent, Michael Dukakis, and portray himself as Mr. Clean *sans* the earring. A local reporter quips, "George Bush coming to Boston and lecturing us on pollution is like Bonnie and Clyde visiting and lecturing on the merits of gun control."

Silly George has literally wrapped himself in the flag in his bid to be Top Banana. At a flag factory he talked about how sales have gone up since Reagan-Bush took over from Carter-Mondale. "We're not going to let them take this away from us," a delirious Vice President told the flag factory throng. Hey, Silly George, Democrats are buried in Arlington National Cemetery, too!

Silly George has already observed Pearl Harbor Day. A slip of the tongue? Saying, "Pearl Harbor Day, September 7th" would be understandable given the rigors the campaign schedule. But Silly George read off a piece of paper, "Today, September 7th, the 47th anniversary of the attack on Pearl Harbor." That's more than a slip of the tongue! In Silly George's penchant for pandering, what better way to rouse a group of veterans than by mentioning Pearl Harbor?

The so-called New Right of the Republican Party has the power to castrate whoever gets the nomination these days. If you don't support a constitutional amendment to make abortion illegal, they'll oppose you. In 1980, Silly George was not in favor of this, and now he says he is. More queasy than usual, Silly George said in the first debate, "And you see — yes, my position has evolved, and it is continuing to evolve, and it is evolving in favor of life." But Republicans don't believe in the Theory of Evolution.

Everyone knew Silly George would have to pick a pro-lifer to make the ticket acceptable to one-issue hard-liners. These crazed faithful threatened to sit out the campaign if the olive branch didn't extend to one of their own. Of course, not supporting Silly George could help elect Mike Dukakis, but that didn't seem to bother them.

This sect of far-out loonies exposed their shallowness when they roundly cheered the selection of J. Danforth Quayle for Veep. Donald Duck would have been acceptable to them, provided the fowl was anti-abortion.

Silly George wants to be the "education President." He'll save Nicaragua from the commies while the majority of school kids can't find Nicaragua on a map. How's Silly George going to be the "education President?" A thousand points of light, of course!

George Bush wants to be President so badly he has sold out the principles he may have once possessed. The man doesn't appear to stand for anything. He's the Gumby Candidate. His eight years as Vice President have made him a bland cipher. A line crafted by a speech writer ("a thousand points of light") or a lame joke fed him by a media wizard seem to make up the persona of George Bush in 1988.

Curious George he's not. Silly George he is.

NJN

Do you get the impression that NJN thinks George Bush is silly? While he was railing against a current and incoming President, I had a more malevolent target in my sights — Morton Downey, Jr. Remember him? He was quite the rage for one brief shining moment in the late '80's.

Fascist Freaks and Jersey Geeks
Morton Downey, Jr., and his groundlings

Charismatic characters have come and gone over the centuries, and have often commanded the blind loyalty of millions. Jesus Christ still has quite a following, but so does Adolph Hitler.

There is an obnoxious talk show host on WWOR-TV named Morton Downey, Jr., a nasty bully and clown who effectively taps into the blue collar *zeitgeist*. His pedestrian "liberals, commies," rave inspires the latent racism/fascism in many a working stiff to surface. His schtick is reminiscent of the Howard Beale character in the movie *Network*, who rallies his audience with the battle cry, "I'm mad as hell, and I'm not going to take it anymore."

We all feel that way on occasion, and if the shouting and venting of Mort's live audience is confined to the studio, then he's providing a healthy catharsis. But once they're wired and wild-eyed, the potential exists for their hostility to spill out into the streets. Mort is not Dr. Frankenstein, but his on stage antics could create a collective monster whose wrath could be particularly messy.

His audience consists mainly of young white males in their twenties through early thirties. Underpaid, overtaxed, angry young fellows. I fit into that demographic. I know these guys. We drink in the same bars. I'm one of them. But when I see them on the Downey circus, acting not as individuals but as one crazed entity, they scare me. He eggs them on with salty dialogue, lewd innuendo (not comic bawdiness, just gutter meanness), and they hang on his every word, laugh at every bad joke, and intimidate the guests. It's the talk show equivalent of "Wrestlemania."

The male guests espousing liberal causes are invariably whining nerds, and the feminine guests are usually unfeminine, and as extremist as Downey. Equally unattractive and intractable. Mort rarely lets them complete a sentence, cutting them off with a wisecrack that prompts hoots from the galoots and drowns out the guests' shrill responses. He occasionally throws a guest out of the studio. At these moments the action seems choreographed.

The only thing to be taken seriously is the unconditional positive regard that Mort gets from the mob.

Those who follow blindly have created chaos and carnage from Day One. A Jew once told a Jewish crowd to yell, "Give us Barabbas," and they did. A Spanish Inquisitor told a Spanish crowd, "Torture and kill all those who disagree with our conception of God," and they did. A Brit told a Brit crowd, "Export all the food from Ireland and leave them a potato or two," and they did, in attempted genocide of the Irish race. In this century, Germans told other Germans to kill the Jews, gypsies, Slavs and everyone who was not one of them. And they did.

Morton's targets are very general, and he seems to go after everyone with equal venom. It was admittedly fun to watch him give it to the Klan, American Nazis, and Lyndon LaRouche. In television-land, the bottom line is the buck, and when Mort's ratings fall, he'll be history.

The agitators come and go, but the mob remains, its rage seething just below the surface, periodically exploding. Scapegoats change, but rage is eternal.

JM

Galoots and Yuppies:
extremism in the offense of us all

In these diseased times, even an evening in at the ballpark can become an infuriating experience. Used to be one only had the galoots to contend with — the cursing, roaring, guzzling hooligans who beat each other to a pulp in pursuit of a foul ball. Now there's a new nuisance, creating a two-front assault, adding arrogance to ignorance. The Yuppies have invaded Shea Stadium.

Once the New York Mets became fashionable again, after winning the 1986 *World Series*, many in the seats during weeknight games were seen wearing their own uniforms, far more menacing than Darth Vader's black helmet and cape. Charcoal gray suits and power ties — the mark of the Yuppie.

They don't pay admission; they sit in corporate boxes. They don't seem particularly interested in the game; they are heard discussing the deals made that day, and the plans to screw us tomorrow. A rare sighting is also made of a galoot-turned-Yuppie, who leaps to his feet to hoot and howl, only to have his bellow stifled by his power tie/leash, and the fear that his CEO might have been watching. Evidence that on the evolutionary scale, galoots and Yuppies may be more alike than you think. They've been destroying everything they touch since the dawn of time. They've followed me to the ballpark all the way from grammar school.

I went to parochial grammar and high school. In NYC public schools, your physical safety is often in jeopardy; in Catholic school, you're subject to emotional shock therapy all day, every day. Nevertheless, future Yuppies and galoots rolled with the punches, adapted and thrived, while the sensitive souls were battered in the maelstrom.

The galoots were the bullies; the Yuppies were the sycophants. My grammar school was administered by ineffectual idealists who let the galoots run wild and welcomed the future-Yuppies' ass-kissing. High school was a fascist theocracy administered by folks who were paid half a public school teacher's salary (hence they were scraped from the bottom of the barrel). The galoot subculture survived despite the psychological warfare (their numb skulls were indifferent to what was being done to them), and the Yuppies were furiously advancing their academic careers. Camps and cliques were quickly established, and outsiders were antagonized.

I was thinking about all this while sitting in Shea Stadium last summer, distracted by the Wall Street rogue discussing his schemes in front of me, and the half-bombed bonehead poised to spill his beer behind me. I thought, wouldn't it be nice if they disappeared, leaving only tailored suits and oil cans in their wake? That scenario is unlikely. The galoots and Yuppies often merge, as they did in the Reagan Administration: The prototype of a galoot-Yuppie unholy alliance.

JM

NJN has never been accused of celebrating diversity, but those fans who loved his leftist slant during the early years must have been outraged by this piece, wherein he tells it like it is.

Fat Albert and the Brawley Kid

Who asked Governor Mario Cuomo to take off his "Klan robes?" Who compared the New York State Attorney General to Adolph Hitler? Who said the state was being run by the Mafia, the Ku Klux Klan, and the Irish Republican Army? The answer: Reverend Al Sharpton, and lawyers Alton Maddox and C. Vernon Mason, also known as The Three Stooges. (Posthumous apologies to Moe, Larry and Curly.)

In November 1987, a 16-year-old black girl named Tawana Brawley claimed to have been raped by six white men, one of whom had a badge. However, once she was placed in the hands of the aforementioned trio, the case degenerated into an absurd sideshow.

One defector from the threesome's henchmen, Perry McKinnon, felt compelled to go public when he became convinced the whole thing was a hoax. He quoted Reverend Al as saying, "I don't care about no facts." I doubt his use of the double-negative meant that he really was interested in the facts.

In the course of the case, Governor Cuomo was branded a racist. Attorney Mason referred to Cuomo and "his people," a derogatory reference to Cuomo's Italian ancestry.

Who are the Governor's "people," Mr. Mason? They're men, women and children who came to America in crowded immigrant ships, with few possessions, who couldn't speak the language, and faced a life of hardship and discrimination. They learned the language, worked 20-hour days, and overcame seemingly insurmountable barriers.

The NAACP which has long fought for equality for blacks, dared to criticize the trio of "advisors" for their baseless accusations. Sharpton promptly labeled them the "National Association for the Advancement of Coon People." Any blacks that challenged their motives were called "Uncle Toms." Mason suggested that Attorney General Robert Abrams was a "sexual pervert," who masturbated while looking at Tawana Brawley's picture.

The strategy of this bigoted trinity: Tie the crime with the three largest white ethnic groups in NY State. Slander them all — the Italians as gangsters, the Irish as terrorists, and the Jews as the money-lenders who control housing, education, etc.

Of course, renowned anti-Semite and all-around hate-monger "Minister" Louis Farrakhan of the Nation of Islam joined the triumvirate's sideshow. Farrakhan lent his legion of bodyguards to Tawana's mother, who was subpoenaed by the grand jury, but instead sought "sanctuary" in his church.

The case was a circus from the start, courtesy of a rotund Rev with a checkered past, and two bitter, sleazy lawyers, spewing hateful bile.

The most outrageous element in the Brawley affair was the reaction of so-called "liberals," who refused to condemn the farcical, inflammatory conduct of the three buffoons, because they were black. Equal rights implies equal treatment.

Sharpton, Maddox and Mason: Go away!

NJN

NJN also had something to say about a slightly more mainstream black public figure.

If Jesse Were White

Mario Cuomo has rather ludicrously stated that, "If Jesse Jackson were white, he'd be elected President." The candidate's detractors cry, "If Jesse were white, he couldn't get elected dog-catcher, given his "Hymietown" slur and past and present associations with Farrakhan, Arafat, and Castro.

Jesse Jackson is not white. So enough already with the "If Jesse were white" diatribes. Jesse Jackson is Jesse Jackson because he's black.

His 1988 Presidential candidacy is unique in the annals of American political history. Still, Jackson has complained vociferously of not being taken seriously by the press and pundits because of his skin pigmentation. He should, however, appreciate the position he's in. He is given oodles of press coverage and his numerous *faux pas* are overlooked precisely because of his hue.

Accept your special situation, Jesse, and come to terms with the double-edged sword of being Jesse Jackson.

NJN

Compelled to write the occasional political piece, I dashed off this little ditty about the influence of celebrities in the electoral process.

Lenny, Ally, and The Duke

You don't care who I want for President, do you?

You shouldn't.

Your decision should be based on the candidate's stance on the issues important to you and yours, and your gut feeling about the man's character.

We all have the right of secret ballot, but I'll share my secret with you after a few words about the tendency of candidates to seek out celebrity endorsements.

It's a pragmatic strategy. More people watch *Entertainment Tonight* than *Meet The Press*. When I was a teenager, William Shatner hawked Promise Margarine on the tube. When Mom sent me to the supermarket and I saw margarine on her shopping list, I bought Promise because it came recommended by Captain Kirk.

The *New York Daily News* recently listed celebrities who are supporting candidates. I gleaned the following from a cursory reading of the text:

· *Better actors vote for Democrats.*
(e.g., Jack Nicholson and Meryl Streep for Democrats; Chad Everett and Lynda Carter for Republicans).

· A surprising number of women and blacks are voting for Republicans. Shame on you, Joans Collins and Rivers, Muhammad Ali and ***O.J. Simpson***. Your sisters and brothers *sans* the big bucks won't be helped by four more years of political elephantitis.

· Pat Robertson has the most eclectic group of supporters: Roy Rogers and Dale Evans, Pat Boone, Rocky Graziano, Rosie Grier, and Mr. T. With endorsements like those, as Mt. T is fond of saying, "I pity the fool."

I would have voted for Bruce Babbitt for three reasons:

1.) He has a marvelous sense of humor, but a deadpan delivery that often confuses his audience. He doesn't look, sound, or act like a funny guy, but I was tuned in to his offbeat wit, and howled heartily. And toward the end of his campaign, when he kept leaping to his feet during debates, he was truly doing "stand-up."

2.) When the candidates were asked the stupid question, "What's your favorite beverage?" He answered, "Beer."

3.) When seeing his wife for the first time after a week's separation, he said, not knowing a microphone was nearby, "Hattie, I'm horny."

And a funny, horny, beer-drinking Democrat is exactly what the country needs!

Since Babbitt is no longer in the running, I hereby formally endorse Michael Dukakis for President. Not because of his inspiring oratory and overwhelming charisma, or the fact that we Northeastern liberals should stick together, but simply because he is supported by Leonard Nimoy and Ally Sheedy. I'm a major Trekker, and have a major crush on the magnificent Miss Sheedy, and those are the bases for my decision.

They're as good reasons as any, considering the field from which we must choose. I wholeheartedly agree with the late H.L. Mencken, who wrote:

It is my firm conviction, reached after long experience, profound pondering and incessant prayer, that no man who is worth a hoot will ever be President of the United States hereafter. We are doomed to suffer an endless procession of quacks, until, that is, the republic blows itself up.

JM

We conclude 1988 with NJN's favorite piece of mine. I must say it is rather insightful for a lad, who, at the time, was putting away a liter of booze a day, with beer chasers.

The Legend of Johnnie Walker

There was a disturbing full-page ad in a major magazine recently. It shows a rear-view of two bikini-clad women jogging on a beach. The caption reads:

He loves my mind.
AND he drinks Johnnie Walker.

And in small print below that:

Good taste is always an asset.

An **ass**et! There is nothing subliminal about that ad. There's also no truth in it. I've sampled Johnnie Walker and just about every other fluid whose active ingredient is ethanol, and girls with assets like those haven't been knocking down my door.

Apart from being utterly unrealistic, there is also something immoral about romanticizing a potentially lethal drug, suggesting that consumers of said chemical will drive fancy cars, be the Big Men of their respective campuses, and have intercourse with beautiful women. Kids are urged not to submit to peer pressure regarding drugs and alcohol, but the admen go unchecked spreading dangerous lies.

You can't watch a ballgame without being deluged by dozens of beer commercials. The frosty can or bottle being removed from the cooler, moisture glistening on its surface. Jocks and blondes exchanging quips and innuendo. They make drinking seem very appealing, and it does have its appeal. (For the record, I am not a prohibitionist. I drink, and am aware of the risks, and at this point remain willing to take them.)

The most unintentionally funny beer commercial is the one with the jokers sitting around in the woods, and one says, "It doesn't get any better than this." The poor slobs. It's a profoundly depressing realization, and for many, a profoundly depressing truth.

My brew of choice is advertised by a famous Aussie, who proclaims with a cocky smirk, "It's Australian for beer, mate." Well, Foster's Lager and all other brews both foreign and domestic can also be Australian for obesity, the runs, cirrhosis, vomiting, bleeding hemorrhoids, thunderous flatulence, and a score of other medical woes.

And an overweight beer guzzler who runs to the john every three minutes and can't stop farting is not a turn-on to women.

JM

1987

This was a mostly NJN year. I contributed only the sporadic paragraph, and only two of those are worthy of inclusion in this anthology.

NJN writes of Ron and Nancy in this first piece. Note that what was being said about Nancy Reagan is similar to what has been said of Hillary Clinton. Bossy broads are a bi-partisan breed, it would seem.

Ron, Nancy, Senility, and The Citizenry

A circus freak show courtesy of the White House — that's what the Presidential press conferences have become, thanks to the President's tendency to not know which end is up.

I'm reminded of Reagan's statement in 1980, when he was a mere lad of 69, that he would be willing to submit to annual tests for senility. Said Ron, "If I were President and had any feeling at all that my capabilities had been reduced before a second term, I would walk away."

The fresh face in the Reagan White House is Howard Baker. The former Senate Majority leader is an intelligent, genial man, the antithesis of his predecessor, Donald Regan. A week before he was tapped to resurrect the Reagan Presidency, Baker told an editor of the *Miami Herald* that Reagan often wore a "blank expression" when conversation turned to things discussed two week's before. Unfortunately Baker's characteristic candor vanished after a day as Reagan's Chief of Staff. "I've never seen Ronald Reagan more energetic, more fully engaged, more in command," said Baker.

Come on, Howard! What do you take us for? We are asked to believe that Reagan at 76, recovering from major prostate and cancer surgeries, has undergone a miraculous metamorphosis and is now a fusion of Lee Iacocca and Captain Kirk?

Ronald Reagan has what is reputed to be the toughest, most demanding job in the world. That is, if you do what the job description dictates. Republican lackeys running around saying, "Reagan's Reagan again," or "The Gipper's back!" is quite unsettling. The Gipper shouldn't be back; he should never have left. The President cannot afford to land on *Fantasy Island*, or wherever Ol' Dutch retreated to while Ollie North and Poindexter ran roughshod through the halls of government.

Then there's Nancy: Some say she's the *de facto* President of the United States. Sheila Tate, Mrs. Reagan's former press secretary says, "Her agenda is Ronald Reagan and that's it."

Ironically, it's the conservative press that have painted Mrs. Reagan as a powerful ogre with the reins of government firmly in her grasp. Their main quibble is that Nancy was not elected by anyone. But, neither was Chief of Staff Regan, whom she allegedly ousted, singlehandedly. The arrogant Wall Streeter, by his own boasting, was calling the shots in the White House.

The President's boosters, by implicating his wife in Don Regan's ousting, are adding to Reagan's much deserved reputation of being "out of touch." The tired excuses of Reagan being ill-advised, or unduly influenced by moderates, are beginning to ring pathetic. Ronald Reagan is a big boy. If he's the great leader he's purported to be, how can so-called non-believers be controlling his agenda? How could he be dominated by his wife? Leadership by

TelePrompt*Her*?

What's relevant is not that Nancy might be in charge, or that Don Regan was. It's that President Reagan wasn't and should have been. Reagan's glib approach to governing is responsible for countless deceptions and fiascos.

Recent polls have indicated noticeable chinks in the President's *Teflon*. Nevertheless, he's still personally popular. It's the "lost boy in the zoo" syndrome — the American public pats the President on the head and reassures him that they still love him, despite his incompetence.

Good news, though: Reagan will not be on the 1988 ticket, and the citizenry is less likely to cuddle to George Bush.

NJN

Well, they did cuddle to Georgie, but only for one term. Next is NJN's observations on Ollie North. I remember watching Ollie testify before Congress from a barstool in my local haunt, and witnessing two old geezers almost come to blows in the "patriot or criminal" debates that were raging that summer. It all seems so long ago. The faces change, but hypocrisy, like the proverbial old soldier, never dies.

The Contemptuous Conservative

"Sanctified by authority and armed with power, error and usurpation bid defiance to truth and right."
— Josiah Quincy, 1774

Lieutenant Colonel Oliver North, American hero? That's what the conservatives would have us believe.

Big deal, he shred a little evidence, destroying government property. So what if, by his own admission, he lied to Congress. A trifling concern, this circumventing of the Constitution.

Ah, the US Constitution. Parties celebrating its 200th birthday abound across the land. The conservative minions, who discreetly endorsed the clandestine government of North, Poindexter and associates, are out in the forefront of the Constitution's bicentennial celebration. Adorned in patriotic regalia, waving miniature flags, and getting misty as Kate Smith sings "God Bless America."

What has Ronald Reagan, patriotism incarnate, said on the matter of subordinates running amok behind his back? Very little. He's positively aglow now that the televised hearings are history, and he's in no danger of being sent up Nixon River. Rear Admiral John Poindexter testified that he never informed the President of the diversion of Iranian arms profits to the Nicaraguan contras. Once again, the President's profound ignorance was confirmed.

The lesson to be learned in the Iran-Contra mess got lost somewhere. It's not that Reagan was spared being removed from office. This wasn't likely to happen to the country's grandfather, even if he was directly linked to the scandal. Rather, it's been the President's silence throughout the avalanche of revelations from his insubordinate underlings. North and Poindexter were deceitful, allegedly keeping their boss in the dark, and making him appear to be a hapless fool. Where was Reagan's indignation; his sense of outrage? Why didn't he come down hard on this reprehensible behavior and set a moral tone the country could be proud of? Instead, he allowed talk of pardons for North and Poindexter to fester.

At the height of the hearings, where was the President? On the road, peddling a package of economic panaceas he called "golden oldies." Oldies, yah; golden, nah!

NJN

I approached the Iran-Contra affair, and two other scandals-du-jour, from a different angle than NJN.

Three Beautiful Girls Three

The common denominator in the three major scandals of the last few months is a stock character in most sleazy melodramas: A beautiful, but dangerous, femme fatale.

SHE was there with the middle-aged brats who traded in their toy guns for the genuine article.

SHE was there with the nerdish fundamentalist who wanted to control what you do behind closed doors, while he did everything with anyone, and milked the masses out of millions in the process.

SHE was there with a would-be President, whose mimicry of JFK extended beyond the political arena.

Fawn Hall, Jessica Hahn, and Donna Rice are the real winners in their respective controversies: Watch the six-figure book contracts, the television docudramas, and the appearances on Phil and Oprah. In a short time all the brouhaha will be forgotten, the names and events only minor footnotes in the pageant of history, but these girls will surely make a bundle as quickly as they can, assuring that their future obscurity wil be reasonably comfortable.

Are these girls victims of a patriarchal society? Shameless gold-diggers selling their souls with their impressive bods? I submit we shouldn't be too hard on these sexy capitalists. They simply have used, and will continue to use, their God-given gifts to commercial advantage. And this is, I'm sure you'll agree, the American way.

JM

I believe that last piece defined the Mannion "fluff" article. With not much to say about anything, reeking of alcohol and insouciance, I cranked out snide little wisecracking pieces exuding nothing but arch detachment.

NJN comments on Jerry Falwell — remember him? — a ubiquitous late '80's big mouth? — in a recurring segment of vignettes he called. . .

Progressive Potpourri

Caught Up In The Rapture

As a nation, we've recognized the danger of driving under the influence of alcohol. However, we have not addressed the hazards of born-again Christians behind the wheel.

Jerry Falwell, a staunch supporter of the President and now a George Bush backer, on "The Rapture":

"You say, 'What's going to happen on this earth when The Rapture occurs?' You'll be riding along in an automobile;

you'll be the driver, perhaps. You're a Christian. There will be several people in the automobile with you; maybe someone who is not a Christian. When the trumpet sounds, you and the other born-again believers in that automobile, will be instantly called away. You will disappear, leaving behind only your clothing and physical things that cannot inherit eternal life. The unsaved person or persons in the automobile will suddenly be startled to find that the car is moving along without a driver and suddenly somewhere crashes. Other cars on the highway driven by believers will suddenly be out of control and stark pandemonium will occur on that highway and every highway in the world where Christians are called away from the driver's wheel."

"Put a Non-Believer Behind The Wheel" should be the next slogan drilled into the American mind-set.

Falwell's 1,000 Year Plan

Jerry Falwell says:

"We believe if Jesus comes today, and no one knows the day or the hour when the Lord is coming, but if he came today then there is at least 1,007 years to be lived out on this planet. Seven years of Tribulation, 1,000 years of the Kingdom Reign of Christ, The Millennium. So no one can destroy the planet for at least 1,007 years. If Jesus was to come 10 years from today, then add that 10 years to the 1,007 and obviously there are 1,017 years of use, and so on. So we don't need to march out in the streets with the peace-niks and the freeze-niks, nor do we have to go to bed wondering if someone's going to push the button and destroy the planet between now and sunrise."

How reassuring. Disturbingly, the President of the free world has voiced, on several occasions, his concurrence with the radical-religious in their belief in an eventual Rapture, Tribulation, and Millennium.

If Ronald Reagan digests such religious rigmarole,

how can he be expected to consummate an arm's treaty with the Soviets? But alas, Reagan also "believes" in balanced budgets.

Hangings In The White House

When Ronald Reagan entered the White House for the first time as President, one of his first executive decisions was which of his predecessors to hang for all the world to see.

The President selected the portraits of Jefferson, Lincoln, Taft, Coolidge, and Eisenhower to be hung in the Cabinet Room. One can understand Jefferson and Lincoln — they're old, uncontroversial favorites. Eisenhower, similarly, is a logical choice for a Republican. After all, there's not much more to choose from. Teddy Roosevelt, a Republican, was also a progressive social activist, anathema to the backward Reaganauts of today.

Reagan took a page right out of the Partisan's Bible by hanging GOP Presidents Taft and Coolidge.

Suffice it to say, out of our 40 Presidents, few can be considered men of greatness. Taft's mega-distinction is being the fattest president in history, weighing in at 353 lbs., and becoming Chief Justice of the Supreme Court in 1921, nine years after his one-term Presidency.

Calvin Coolidge made his mark on history by accomplishing, and saying, nothing. During Silent Cal's "Keep Cool with Coolidge" 1924 campaign, a story has it that a reporter called out:

"Mr. President, what do you think about Prohibition?"

"No comment," replied Coolidge.

"Will you say something about unemployment?"

"No."

"Will you tell us your views about the world situation?"

"No."

"About your message to Congress?"

"No."

Distraught in eliciting nary a peep from the reticent President, the reporter walked away, at which point Coolidge called out, "Wait! Now remember, don't quote me."

Ronald Reagan has also had glowing words for Herbert Hoover. Conservative revisionist historians have sought to portray Hoover as a victim of circumstances, who acted forthrightly and without rashness in the face of the worst Depression in world history. Ex-President Coolidge, who had a way with words, remarked in 1932, "The country is not in good condition." Indeed, Coolidge and Hoover typified the bloodless bureaucrat, impotent as the nation sank deeper and deeper into hopelessness.

Who is hung in the White House may be a portent of things to come. Reagan is habitually lazy like Taft, notorious for dozing off during meetings. He mimics Silent Cal when confronted by the press. And he's a heartless buffoon to many, in the tradition of Herbert Hoover.

Pope-pourri: Waldheim's Roman Holiday

What's Pope John Paul II doing these days? He's the spiritual czar of Roman Catholicism and is recognized as an infallible moral authority by Catholics across the globe. Why then did he compromise his lofty reputation by granting an audience to an unrepentant former Nazi, Austrian President Kurt Waldheim?

Apologists for the Holy Father say that he is a person of infinite forgiveness — after all, he did meet with the man who almost killed him in an assassination attempt.

Waldheim, however, did not request a meeting with

the Pope to seek absolution of his sins. He remained, as always, arrogant in the face of his deeds, with the smug countenance of a hack politician at peace with his slimy life. Nor did the Pontiff treat Waldheim as a grievous sinner. Instead, he lavished praise on the former UN Secretary General, ironically calling him a man who was "always devoted to securing the peace."

The crux of the Pope-Waldheim tête-à-tête is its detrimental impact on Catholic-Jewish relations. The Pope has grossly erred, and shattered his credibility and that of the insular, parochial, aging all male decision-making body that operates behind the gold-plated walls of Vatican City.

NJN

Another fluff piece from me, with slightly more substance.

Rated "O"

The US Catholic Conference Department of Communications has its own ratings system of the "moral suitability" of movies. Roughly equivalent with the secular ratings system as follows: A-1=G; A-2=PG; A-3=R; A-4=R "with reservations," and O= "morally objectionable."

Here are the US Catholic Conference's reviews of two popular summer movies:

They give *The Untouchables* an A-3. It's a great movie, but a brutally violent one. One would think they might find the savagery in the film "morally objectionable."

Dragnet, a marginally entertaining and inoffensive summer comedy, is rated "O." I think there are two reasons for this severe critique:

1.) The villain of the piece is a Roman-collared reverend (not a Catholic priest) who secretly heads an evil cult called PAGAN. This must have upset the other men-in-black.

2.) One brief scene has Tom Hanks's character in bed with his girlfriend. He reaches for a box of condoms at his bedside, and, finding it empty, refrains from love-making.

DeNiro as Al Capone cracking open another man's skull with a baseball bat in graphic detail is not morally offensive, but the notion of an unmarried couple practicing safe sex is a moral outrage!

The US Catholic Conference Department of Communications has a right to its opinion, just as this former altar boy has a right to his. Five hundred years ago the Church tortured and killed those who disagreed with them. I am absolutely convinced that if they could still get away with it, they'd still be doing it.

Thank God times have changed.

JM

Finally, from our second year in business, here are some more NJN short pieces.

Progressive Potpourri

All In The Family

In the aftermath of the Gary Hart-Donna Rice "weekend of innocence," the remaining Presidential hopefuls, Democrat and Republican alike, are displaying wives and children in abundance on the campaign trail, in an effort to present voters with an aura of familial bliss and rock-solid character.

Rep. Richard Gephardt, with his cartoon-like features, teamed up with his wife in the "Dick and Jane Show." Yes, Mrs. Gephardt is named Jane. Gephardt answered the question of whether he committed adultery forthrightly, even eagerly, as if it were germane to the campaign. The issue of adultery was pertinent to Gary Hart because his indiscretions were known for years by many Washington insiders and journalists. With squeaky-clean Gephardt, the question was irrelevant.

Senator Joseph Biden has spoken publicly for the first time about the tragic accident that killed his first wife and infant daughter. Similarly, Vice President Bush has talked candidly about the death of his three-year-old daughter from leukemia in 1953.

Divorce, on the other hand, is old news. Ronald Reagan is our first divorced Chief Executive; he is, however, "hopelessly in love" with his second wife. Interestingly, the Republican Party, with its moralistic underpinnings and emphasis on traditional values, has given us not only the first divorced President, but a fractured First Family. Two Reagan kids have written books that reflect poorly on the parental skills of Ron and Nancy.

The President's closest friend, and now a Presidential candidate, Paul Laxalt, is divorced, as is Bob Dole, another contender. Meaningless stuff, were it not for their hypocrisy in championing a lifestyle that they themselves haven't lived. Reagan as the embodiment of "God and Family" is laughable.

P.S. — As Governor of California, Reagan signed into law the most liberal abortion statute in American history, and he's a notorious non-church-goer to boot.

The Laxalt Letter

Is God a Republican? Paul Laxalt thinks so, as his letter of 1984 to prominent evangelists indicates:

Dear Christian Leader:

As chairman of Reagan-Bush '84, the President's authorized campaign committee, I am writing to ask you to play a significant role in what may very well be the most pivotal election of this century. President Reagan, as you know, has made an unwavering commitment to traditional values, which I know you share. In addition, he has, on several occasions, articulated his own spiritual convictions.

As leaders under God's authority, we cannot afford to resign to idle neutrality in an election that will confirm or silence the President that has worked so diligently on your behalf.

Caveat Emptor

Alexander ("I'm in control here") Haig, former Secretary of State and current Presidential candidate, when asked it he thought the President had read his book, *Caveat*, detailing his days in the Reagan White House, replied that he "hoped so," adding, "That's why I made it a short book."

Newts and Quayles

After the Tower Commission published its findings, the President addressed the nation in vintage fashion, taking "full responsibility" for the Iran-Contra debacle. Newt Gingrich of Georgia called Reagan's performance "historic," adding, "A century from now, I can imagine a staffer pulling it out when a President makes a really big mistake, and saying, 'This is how great Presidents respond when they blow it.'" Senator Dan Quayle of Indiana trumpeted, "The Gipper's back! He's learned his lesson and is ready to move on."

Days of Whine and Noses

Mayor Ed Koch of NYC, presiding over a rampantly corrupt administration, and John Cardinal O'Connor, Vicar of NYC, have teamed to produce a book and video about their intertwining escapades, entitled, *His Eminence and Hizzoner*. How modest! May I suggest the alternate title of *Days of Whine and Noses*, in light of their loudmouthed antics and prominent probosci.

My Heart Bleeds For. . .

. . . multimillionaire Donald Trump who has been complaining that "his city" is being ruined by street peddlers, the poor schleps selling cheap jewelry and umbrellas on NYC sidewalks.

What a Difference Three Decades Make!

1986:

Lt. Col. Ollie North takes the Fifth Amendment, exercising his right to do so, and is extolled as a patriot.

1956:

John Smith, member of the Screen Actors' Guild (SAG President that year was Ronald Reagan), takes the Fifth and is blacklisted for life, branded a "communist."

Oral Report: God as Kingpin

As you read this, the fate of evangelist and spiritual extortionist Oral Roberts, may have been already decided. Roberts warned his followers that March is the deadline God has given him for raising eight million dollars. "We're at the point where God could call Oral Roberts home," he said, admonishing each member of his flock to send him $100.

The Greatest Miracle

Jimmy Swaggart is a colorful evangelist. He sweats and cries a lot on the tube in "genuine sincerity."

Swaggart has said of Mahatma Gandhi, "Gandhi was one of the most noble men to ever live, yet as we know he died without God." He said of Catholicism, the religion of which his is a mere spin-off, "I don't see how a nun, a priest, or Catholic layman can remain in this tradition as they become familiar with the Bible and realize that the Catholic tradition is in complete contradiction to the will of God."

Watching his program, *A Study in The Word*, is great entertainment. One amusing encounter occurred during a panel discussion on miracles when Swaggart spoke of what was "the greatest miracle in history," that of God parting the

Red Sea to allow Moses and the Israelites passage out of Egypt. A panel member said that as the sea parted, it "coagulated" into an icy mass. Swaggart questioned this freezing hypothesis on the grounds that the Holy Land was too sultry to sustain frost.

I'd just like to say to Rev. Swaggart that if God Almighty wanted to, he could certainly make water freeze, even in desert heat. And another thing, Jimmy: I was also under the impression that the greatest miracle was the resurrection of Christ. But then again, I was raised a Roman Catholic and am clearly out of the loop in such matters.

NJN

Not long after this, Swaggart, who denounced many to eternal damnation, was caught in a hotel with a prostitute. They weren't "doing it," however, he was merely masturbating while watching her engage in some erotic antics. Old news that we've all heard before, but it bears repetition.

Epilogue
1986
"and the first shall be last . . ."

Just in case you're the type of browser who'll look at the first few pages of a book in the store before buying it, we decided to save our first year for the last chapter of this book. Our "hip, conversationalist style," as one reader derisively described my work, was a shrill infant in comparison to the sophisticated maturity it would attain. For the historical record, however, we nevertheless present our early years. Under our first, unintentionally ironic subtitle, "Come Now. . .Let Us Reason Together," we took our hesitant baby steps on the path toward Eternity.

Environmental Ennui in the White House

It needn't be a conservative versus liberal argument; a Republican versus Democratic one. But that's what it has become. Environmental pollution is surely a common enemy to us all. It's how to tackle this environmental impasse where the battle lines are drawn.

The sorry statistics don't lie: The government's Office of Technology Assessment has appraised that in a minimum of 10,000 locales through the US, hazardous waste sites pose an imminent health threat. The General Accounting Office reports that an excess of 375,000 "pools of pollutants" exist. Yes, years of amassing steel drums laden with toxins have finally caught up with us, as rust and erosion introduce the poisons into the earth, contaminating the water sources.

Yet the EPA has less than 1,000 dump sites on its priority list for immediate action. Environmental guidance has been tossed aside in favor of deregulatory measures aimed at expanding business fertility. The so-called Reagan conservative ideology trumpets that we should spare the taxpayers a few dollars. Conservation of cash-- period!

Of course, the pitiful irony is that studies undertaken both privately and in government indicate astronomical costs of delousing the environment several years in the future, if remedial action is not taken now.

For the record, it must be said that the EPA's integrity has been greatly enhanced with the appointments of William Ruckelshaus and his successor, Lee Thomas. When Ronald Reagan assumed the gigantic task of his Presidency, he appointed a Republican Party fund-raiser, Anne Burford, to run the EPA. She, in turn, was instrumental in the selection of Rita Lavelle to oversee the Superfund toxic-waste clean-up.

What ensued in a flurry of greed, corruption, and stupidity was Lavelle's conviction of perjury for denying EPA involvement with some of the country's most horrible polluters. Burford, on the other hand, was charged with contempt of Congress for refusing to submit requested documentation. Simultaneously, the Reagan budgetary agenda was lopping off one-quarter of the EPA's funding and one-fifth of its staff.

What's to be the legacy of this prevailing philosophy? Some of the damage is already irreparable. Conditions worsen with each inactive day. What remains is hope -- hope that the short-sightedness of today does not engulf us in a swamp of squalor. After all, we are merely squatters on this land; future generations will tread the same sod and breathe the same air as us. They deserve that opportunity.

NJN

There you have it--the front page article of the premiere issue of The Progressive Pragmatist. Uncharacteristically well-documented, if a bit didactic. What follows is the "hip, conversationalist style" which made us infamous.

Seduced by the Fourth Stooge

Right-wingers are inclined to brand all liberals as communists. This is, of course, an asinine notion. I tend to label all right-wingers as fascists. This is, of course, somewhat less asinine.

Yes, the lamentable J.E. Carter was instrumental in fueling the feeling that Republicans are Real Men, and liberal Democrats are castrated wimps. As a liberal Democrat with a fully functional pair of testicles in my scrotum, I assure you this prejudice simply ain't so.

Moe, Larry, Curly. . . Ronny. The 4th Stooge. Years ago he was a smiling spokesman for a major corporation, a friendly face and perfect pitch-man. He hasn't changed; he just croons for a new cause -- the new breed of conservatives and their bizarre definition of American Values.

Used to be there was a healthy sense of patriotism -- fierce individualism, sympathy and support for the underdog, and contempt for the bland bureau-rats who destroy everything they touch.

"My country, right or wrong," is wrong.

"America -- love or leave it," is baloney.

Right is right and wrong is wrong, and if politicians are wrong, we have the right to vote the bums out. That's America, buddy!

I'm not as fearful as I used to be, for I've observed that folks seem to be rallying around Reagan himself. He is a personally popular bloke. The 4th Stooge is conning 'em, but he's on his way out, and the other dudes don't have the same appeal. If we can survive two more years without Vietnam II south of the border, or the Big Bang II that'll destroy us all, we may just survive as a species for another few centuries.

The valuable lesson to learn from Reagan is that the Presidency seems to have degenerated into a figurehead office, much like the Queen of England. He's just an old actor playing the role of a lifetime. And he's still a bad actor; this performance makes his turn in *Hellcats of the Navy* seem like Oscar material.

One quick word about the fundamentalists, core Reagan supporters. Specifically, this is for fundamentalist women.

Ladies:

The literal interpretation of the Bible puts you in a second-class citizenry that is anachronistic in these enlightened times. Read the scriptures and see the horrors women endured. Look at the Islamic fundamentalists: They keep their womenfolk veiled and degraded. If American fundamentalists could get away with similar chicanery, rest assured they would.

JM

Inflammatory, but I did predict George Bush's one-term Presidency. And didn't a political scientist write a book about Reagan titled, "The Role of a Lifetime?" Obviously, he was a Progressive Pragmatist reader.

Please note that NJN was the first to publicly criticize John Cardinal O'Connor, though I came to be known as the Cardinal-basher of the team. Bless us Father, for we have sinned. . .

Presidential Pew-berty

Throughout the Presidential contest of 1984, when America witnessed its first woman on a major national ticket, politics became inexplicably woven with religion. While much of the religious rumble emanated from the fundamentalist faction, the Catholic Church also raised its voice.

Geraldine Ferraro, three-term Congresswoman from Queens, New York, was Walter Mondale's running mate. She was a Catholic, and pro-choice on the abortion issue. This did not sit well with her Archbishop, John Cardinal O'Connor. O'Connor had habitually made it clear that, in his humble opinion, abortion was the most important concern facing humankind. "No need is more crucial than the protection of the rights of the unborn," is his credo. He had never, to date, so blatantly entered the political fray.

The situation confronting him was unique. Never before on the national level was there a Catholic woman espousing a position contrary to Church teaching. O'Connor would not sit idly by. He professed, "I do not see how a Catholic in good conscience can vote for an individual expressing himself or herself in favor of abortion." Of course, he denied that he was instructing his flock on how to vote. Nonetheless, his proclamation left "good conscience" Catholics with little choice but to vote for the pro-life Republicans.

While Bishop of Scranton, O'Connor was a registered Republican. On the traditional courtesy call extended by New York's Archbishop to Presidential candidates every four years, the Cardinal emerged with President Reagan all smiles, effusive with praise. When he hosted Walter Mondale, his countenance was decidedly solemn. It was clear, Cardinal O'Connor preferred Ronald Reagan.

Most disturbing was O'Connor's downright hostility exhibited toward Ferraro. He maintained that Ferraro had misrepresented Church positions by claiming that Catholics could hold diverse opinions on the abortion question. Dealing with a woman seemed more than some of these prelates could handle. Bishop Timlin of Scranton termed Ferraro's stand "absurd" and "dangerous." Ironically, he later admitted to being unaware of his two Senator's positions on the question. Both were pro-choice, and both were Republican.

One can only hazard a guess as to what O'Connor has up his vestments as the 1988 campaign looms. Will he again choose to vilify a particular candidate and seek to make the race solely a referendum on abortion? Will he again ignore the issues of poverty and the threat of nuclear holocaust? If he does, all Catholics, indeed all Americans, will be the sorry victims.

NJN

I briefly had a column in The Progressive Pragmatist called "Gentleman Jim Speaks." The clever logo featured a desktop with an old-fashioned typewriter, a cigar smoldering in an ashtray, and a can labeled "XXX." (I was a bottle-a-day boozehound in those days.) NJN curiously included the disclaimer "The opinions expressed are solely those of the author," as if to distance himself from his partner in a two-man operation.

Gentleman Jim Speaks!
Political Perversity in New York

A positive result of Watergate is that it made the citizenry suspicious and skeptical of politicians as a species. When a guy or gal spends $9 million for a job that pays $75,000 and tells you he wants to "give something back," he should automatically be suspect.

Most successful pols end up owing the wrong people many favors. The truly dedicated, incorruptible characters rarely rise above dog catcher.

In our alleged two-party system, the Democrats enact social programs that do some good for the commoners, but not at the expense of the Big Boys who pull the strings.

The Republicans, more honest in a scummy way, make no bones about their "screw you" attitude: *We're here and you're there and keep your distance pals, or we'll sic the dogs on ya.*

In New York City, there was a recent corruption scandal, more widespread than the foul play of the Tammany Hall days. From his City Hall sanctuary, dome-headed Ed Koch, who you non-New Yorkers know as a walking stereotype, says, "I had no idea all these guys I've known for over 20 years were crooks. But the buck stops here, and I'm accountable."

So will you do the noble thing, Mr. Mayor, and fall on your sword (or as Queens Boro Prez Donald Manes did, your kitchen knife)? Of course you won't, Eduardo.

You can't survive forever with your Borscht Belt schtick. You're as transparent as Saran Wrap, buddy, we see right through you.

I grew up here, still live here, and love this town. But, Mr. Mayor, you're killing it. You've allowed the big shot realtors to evict the working poor from their hovels, forcing them into the streets. The same hovels are rented and sold to sleazy young Yuppies who pay two grand a month for a claustrophobic cube to crawl into. You've got to be quite well off or dirt poor to live on Manhattan Island these days. The middle class is being run out of town, and as a result, the city will die. Not with a bang, but with a whine. The nasal obnoxious whine of Ed Koch, murderer of Manhattan.

JM

Monkey Business Then and Now

Some 60 years ago, the most (in)famous example of fundamentalist tomfoolery was acted out on a county courthouse in Dayton, Tennessee. This was, of course, the notorious Monkey Trial, wherein mild-mannered high school teacher John T. Scopes, was accused of violating one of the wildest laws to ever make it into the books.

He was defended by the foremost progressive pragmatist of his day, Clarence Darrow, and prosecuted by William Jennings Bryan, three-time Presidential candidate and backwoods bellower extraordinaire. He represented the powers that be who were advocating, with no room or discussion or debate, the literal interpretation of the Bible.

Consider the Book of Genesis: How can one couple (Adam and Eve) with two sons (Cain and Abel), one of whom killed the other, populate the entire planet without indulging in some pretty raunchy incestuous pornography?

The logic continues to deteriorate and the contradictions are fruitful and multitudinous. Consider the Old Testament's Yahweh -- a cranky old cuss if ever there was one. And Christ of the New Testament -- love everybody, including your enemies. A philosophy that'll get you stabbed in the back every time. Look what happened to the fella who said it.

After several thousand years and as many translations, it cannot be taken literally. Translators will consciously or unconsciously add their attitudes and prejudices to their translations.

In its original form, Genesis is a poem -- a lyrical attempt to explain the unexplainable. It's as mythic as the Greco-Roman tales of that naughty crew on Mount Olympus. Dingalings will tell you it is fact, and suggest that those who disagree are gonna burn, baby, burn. Pride is allegedly a deadly sin, and these dudes are sinfully and smugly secure of their own salvation.

A note to you yahoos: I am intolerant of your intolerance. I am prejudiced against your bigotry, and I shall raise up my voice to shout you clowns down at every opportunity. Sixty years ago you had Mencken to contend with. Well, boys and girls, it's 1986 and Gentleman Jim is here!

JM

Talk about hubris! The jury is still out on that one, but time will tell. Eh, my friends?

Our political ravings in our first year are almost too embarrassing to reprint. Of course we will if this book is a bestseller and the general public clamors for a sequel. So I thought I'd include a piece that NJN loved so much he inserted in two issues. Submitted for your perusal: The last letter President Andrew Jackson received from his mother. File it away under --

Mother Knows Best.

Andrew, if I should not see you again I wish you to remember and treasure some things I have already said to you: In this world you will have to make your own way. To do that you must have friends. You can make friends by being honest, and you can keep them by being steadfast. You must keep in mind that friends worth having will in the long run expect as much from you as they give you. To forget an obligation or be ungrateful for a kindness is a base crime, not merely a fault or a sin but an actual crime. Men guilty of it sooner or later suffer the penalty. In personal conduct be always polite, but never **obsequious**. *No one will respect you more than you esteem yourself. Avoid quarrels as long as you can without yielding to imposition. But sustain your manhood always. Never bring a suit of law for assault and battery or for defamation. The law affords no remedy for such outrages that can satisfy the feelings of a true man. Never wound the feelings of others. Never brook wanton outrage upon your own feelings. If ever you have to vindicate your feelings or defend your honor, do it calmly. If angry at first, wait till your wrath cools before you proceed.*

Now I know where NJN picked up the word "obsequious," which appears at least half a dozen times in this book (almost as much as "blowhard")! Here's another "title-first" article, with substance being a relatively minor concern.

Reagan III: The Wrath of Ron

The Republican Party was responsible for the constitutional amendment limiting a President to two terms, in an effort to thwart another FDR-style reign. Now they want to repeal the 22nd Amendment to keep the 4th Stooge in the White House. These crackpots are probably the same dudes who want to carve Ronny's head on Mount Rushmore.

Adolph Hitler seized Germany from Hindenburg, a senile old goat and purely figurehead leader. It can happen here!

Give it a rest, Mr. Reagan. Go back to the ranch. Enjoy your golden years. You deserve a break, and so do we. Leave the Republican Party to stand on its own two feet, and hopefully it will fall flat on its face.

JM

Excuse the mixed metaphor. Great title, though. Don't you think?

Here's an NJN quickie, with a less clever title than the previous piece, I might add!

Hart Transplant

Early in the 1984 Democratic primaries, Senator Gary Hart of Colorado emerged from virtual obscurity as a serious contender for the Presidential nomination.

His successes were largely attributed to the substantial support he received from the newly-discovered voting bloc called Yuppies.

Remarkably, network exit polls revealed that the vast majority of "Yuppies" who cast ballots for Gary Hart in the Democratic primaries would vote for Ronald Reagan in the general election, if Hart's opponent, Walter Mondale, received the nomination.

Paradoxically, the same Gary Hart was rated the most liberal Senator by Americans for Democratic Action (ADA), the litmus test of liberalism.

Yet, the "Yuppie" would vote for Ronald Reagan over Walter Mondale, after enthusiastically backing Gary Hart. They'd vote for a bona fide liberal who looked like Hart, and not an ideological soul-mate with the looks of Fritz Mondale. Instead they'd vote for a man who was the complete antithesis of the man they ardently supported in the primaries.

Draw your own conclusion.

NJN

In journalism school and beyond, well-meaning and not so well-meaning critics warned me that I was fast in danger of becoming a self-parody. Upon reviewing our Progressive Pragmatist infancy, it was clear that I was a self-parody from the get-go. So, it's fitting that I close our final chapter with a piece of unrepentant hip-bombast.

I Object!

While consuming a few cold ones in the local gin mill recently, I overheard a couple of cranky oldsters blasting the late FDR, accusing him of being a Socialist bastard, if not an outright Red. I tried in vain to explain to these crowing old coots that FDR actually preserved democracy as we know it during those dangerous Depression days, when the nation could have swung toward fascism or communism, as many others did.

There is a dark side to passionate patriotism. Certain lunatic lunkheads carry it to overzealous nationalism and xenophobia. Look different and they despise you, disagree with 'em and they'll strike with intent to maim. There's a bully-boy mentality in many American pseudo-patriots, a holier-than-thou smugness and penchant for violence. And yet they're also sheepish camp followers. The fabric of most fascists is 100% wool.

Fascism in America will not arrive in the form of armed insurrection as in so many two-bit banana republics. There is the danger that it could insidiously overtake us in the courts. And with Ron & Co. stacking the deck, we could well be on the road to ruin.

If a Nazi can head the United Nations (Kurt Waldheim), why can't a closet Klansman head the US

Supreme Court? Justice Rehnquist has been accused of supporting illegal wiretapping, condoning the notion of mass arrest, and holding suspects indefinitely without formal charges. He has been accused of insensitivity (some say downright hostility) to the plight of women and minorities. Wild stuff in the land of the free.

If these geeks get their way, then Phil Donahue and I (and you, citizens) are in a hell of a lot of trouble. They'll not only go after the loudmouths in the public eye, but the average joe with a dissenting voice may find himself in grave jeopardy. Even the scribblers of this modest sheet could find themselves swinging from the nearest lamppost.

The US Supreme Court is entering the 21st century with a Chief Justice possessing 19th century values and prejudices. Thanks for nothing, Ronny.

A quick word on the notorious Judge Manion, another of Reagan's brilliant selections. The deans of 40 law schools signed a letter to the powers-that-be, urging that they not accept him on the federal court. They claimed his legal brief contained numerous grammatical and spelling errors, not to mention his association with the John Birch Society.

That his reports are full of spelling errors does not suprise me in the least. Judge Manion can't even spell his last name.

James Mannion

Note the misspelling of "surprise" in the very same sentence where I chastise Judge Manion. I could have corrected that for this edition, but I chose to close with a little self-deprecating irony, to prove that we are, in fact, "regular guys," and not the self-important blowhards some of you may perceive us to be, as you close this little book of ours.

If you enjoyed *America Off-Line*, and are interested in the other titles in the *Cryptic Press* line (and our merchandise line of buttons and bumper stickers), drop us a note to receive a copy of the *Cryptic Press Report.*

Cryptic Press, Inc.
One Riverdale Avenue, Suite 452
Bronx, New York 10463

or E-mail us at --
CrypticKid@aol.com